ANTIQUITIES ACQUIRED

ANTIQUITIES ACQUIRED

The Spoliation of Greece

C. P. BRACKEN

DAVID & CHARLES
NEWTON ABBOT   LONDON
NORTH POMFRET (VT)   VANCOUVER

0 7153 7000 6

Library of Congress Catalog Card Number 74-19779

Set in 11 on 13pt Garamond and printed in
Great Britain by Latimer Trend & Company Ltd Plymouth
for David & Charles (Holdings) Limited
South Devon House Newton Abbot Devon

Published in the United States of America
by David & Charles Inc   North Pomfret
Vermont 05053   USA

Published in Canada by Douglas David & Charles Limited
3645 McKechnie Drive West Vancouver BC

CONTENTS

LIST OF ILLUSTRATIONS

List of Illustrations

INTRODUCTION

Greece has been losing her antiquities for 2,000 years. But never, since Nero looted 500 statues from Delphi, has the rate of loss increased so sharply as during the early years of the last century. It was then that Western Europe woke up to the glory that had been Grecian art and architecture, and then that acquisition by purchase, bribery and influence denuded Greece so swiftly of so many of her remaining treasures.

Under the Byzantine emperors, Greece had sunk into oblivion: in AD 527 began the long silence of history about the country that had once been the most famous in the world. For 700 years she was scarcely mentioned, until the Crusaders and Venetians, fresh from the rape of Constantinople, threw themselves on her to carve out princedoms and duchies, erect trading posts and squabble amongst themselves and with the successors of the tottering Byzantine Empire. Then came the Turks: Mahomet II, the new conqueror of Constantinople, entered Athens in 1455, and a further period of semi-oblivion commenced, broken only by the sporadic incursions of the Venetians. In 1770, Catherine of Russia backed a Greek rising in the Morea against the Turks; it was a miserable and bloody failure.

The next period is characterised by the rise of Ali Pasha, that 'monstrous spawn of despotism', who from his base at Jannina in the Epirus reached out to bring more and more Greek provinces under his murderous though comparatively stable sway. Finally, the Sublime Porte could no longer tolerate the quasi-independence he had achieved: it crushed him.

The Sultan was now faced with the rebellion of the native Greeks: the War of Independence broke out in 1821, to pursue its bloody and vacillating course until the destruction of the Turkish fleet at Navarino by the combined English, French and Russian forces opened the way for an independent Greek state.

Over all these centuries, earthquake and flood, wind and rain threw down, buried or eroded the Greek temples and sculptures; men utilised the debris to build themselves houses, burnt the marbles to make lime for mortar, and melted the bronze to make cooking utensils. The rare visitors recorded something of what was left. But original Greek art and architecture were little known or admired in the West: according to the dictates of the best eighteenth-century taste, Roman adaptations and remains were the ones to be copied and coveted: in the latter half of that century, ancient marbles from Italy—and fakes—flooded to the West in a furore for collecting classical art, and no one thought of returning from the 'Grand Tour' without specimens of sculpture, coins or vases.

Yet the often poor copies of Greek statuary in Rome, and the splendid Doric temples of Paestum and Sicily, had alerted the connoisseurs. In 1755, several of them financed the artists Stuart and Revett on a mission into Greece to record its art and architecture; the first volume of their *Antiquities of Athens* did not, however, come out till 1762, which enabled the French artist Le Roy to steal a march by publishing his somewhat cursory *Ruines des plus beaux monuments de la Grèce* in 1758. The circulation of these and other travelogues and drawings stimulated interest and encouraged travellers to see for themselves. For the English there was an additional reason to venture eastwards: the Napoleonic wars had virtually closed France and Italy to them: the Grand Tour had to range farther afield and the amateurs of antiquity seek fresh sources of supply. Before long it could be said that no man was accounted a traveller who had not bathed in Sparta's Eurotas and tasted the olives of Attica, while it was an introduction to the best company and a passport to literary distinction to be a member of the Athenian Club and to have scratched one's name upon a column of the Parthenon.

What was understood by 'archaeology' in those days? Contemporary writings lead to the conclusion that the term covered a concern with almost anything related to antiquity. A distinction can be made, however, between the acquisition of antiquities in the field, and the use that was subsequently made of them by scholars, artists, architects and men of taste. It is with the first that this book is concerned.

Field archaeology was still at the open-cast stage and antiquities were culled almost entirely from ground surface; if collectors dug, they simply put the spade in, their aim being to obtain the maximum number of antiquities with the greatest possible speed. A conception of excavation as a means of identifying and noting the successive levels of human occupation of a site hardly entered their heads; they did not seek to reconstruct the buried civilisations of the unrecorded past.

Thus the aims of the collectors who first entered the Grecian field would barely, if at all, be considered archaeological by today's standards. We shall see these aims illustrated in the accounts of the acquisitions: Elgin's mission despoiling Greece to provide England with examples of the best in Greek art and architecture and thereby improve the national taste; Clarke removing a statue from Eleusis to adorn the library of his university for the general edification; Cockerell and his friends measuring and sketching the temples of Aegina and Bassae to train themselves professionally and improve their private taste, whilst creaming each site of its sculpture to sell at a handsome profit, in which aim they are joined by the French consul Fauvel, collecting and dispersing antiquities, half antiquarian, half dealer.

The methods used by the acquirers were equally foreign to today's scientific excavation procedures: they usually neglected to record when and how they discovered their finds, and thus we find Marcellus acquiring a Venus to which could be attached the name of an island, Melos, but little other reliable information; they had no conception of the treasures, material and informational, that could be derived from excavating whole sites like Delos or the Athens Agora, and thus Dubois was content to dig out a few fragments of sculpture at Olympia, leaving the vast spread of buried relics almost untouched.

These leading actors were joined in such pre-archaeology by all the host of lesser depredators with similar aims and methods, picking up sculpture at random and demolishing graves to retrieve only the most desirable contents, so that it was impossible to assign a provenance to most of the trophies they brought back.

This is not to say, though the matter cannot be dealt with in this book, that once such raw material had been scooped up, study of it was neglected by scholars. Ever since Winckelmann had, in the mid-eighteenth century, laid the foundations of the history of ancient art by attempting to place its productions in a chronological sequence, archaeological scholars had been producing descriptive and comparative studies of antique sculpture and architecture, bronzes, vases and terracottas in order to determine how and where the arts had originated, to follow their progress, seek out the poetical and mythological concepts that had guided the artists, and discover and distinguish their artistic and technical procedures. The history of art had, indeed, become the prime object of archaeology, though epigraphy remained indispensable and collections of the Greek and Roman inscriptions that had been removed to the West or copied on the spot were constantly published, accompanied by learned reconstitutions and interpretations; numismatists, whose first concern was often the beauty and comprehensiveness of their collections of coins, none the less did not overlook their interpretative significance; topographers, finally, must not be forgotten, seeking to identify lost classical sites and bring to book the geography of the ancient world.

The impact of the acquisitions on western art and architecture, taste and fashion, is barely touched on in this book; the subject has been fully covered in many publications, the most recent of which is Dr J. Mordaunt Crook's *Neo-Classicism*.

The accounts of the acquisitions are drawn from the contemporary sources mentioned in the Biographical and Bibliographical Index; this also records some of the minor protagonists' booty, though the accounts of their depredations are too casual and contradictory for a general summary to be attempted.

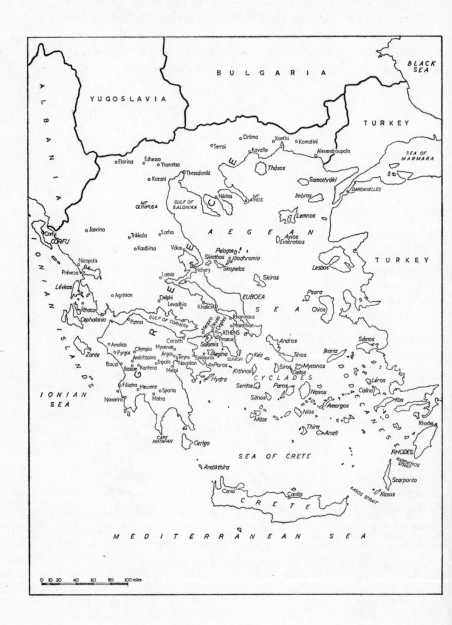

I

GREECE IN 1800

In 1800, mainland Greece was a run-down province of the ram-shackle Ottoman Empire.

Though hardly above a dozen western travellers had visited her over as many years, it was known that remains of her beautiful edifices still existed and that the temple of Minerva—as the Parthenon was then known—still crowned the Acropolis of Athens; sketches and architectural drawings had been published and handed round amongst connoisseurs, and there were rumours of more to come.

But disappointment awaited the traveller who expected to find on the spot troupes of elegant artistes acting the masterpieces of Sophocles or Euripides, or monuments everywhere as consider-able as the Paris Bourse and Westminster Cathedral; the delightful fictions of the classical poets, after playing on his imagination for years, would be rapidly denuded of their charms by the deplor-able realities of Turkish oppression and forgotten, half-buried temples and cities.

Arriving at Athens by sea, the traveller's worst fears would be confirmed when he saw the fate that had overtaken the Piraeus, that once magnificent port whose triple harbour, arsenals, temples and theatres had been celebrated in antiquity. All he would see would be a ruined mole beside which lay a fishing-boat, a cluster of miserable huts on the shore and a monastery standing on the rise above. His first task on landing would be to hire horses to transport himself and his baggage to the town, for there were almost no carriage roads in Greece and consequently no carriages.

The way from the coast lay through olive groves and over a track that followed the broken foundations of Themistocles' Long Walls and was scarcely in better condition. Soon, a closer view of Athens revealed what was little more than a large village dotted with the palms, cypresses and minarets that relieved the monotony of flat roofs covered in pantiles of dusky brown; where the houses straggled out on to the level ground around the Acropolis, their courtyards were large and they were separated by open spaces in which crops ripened and cattle grazed; where tiny jumbled cottages huddled on to the slopes of the citadel, they were linked by narrow lanes and steep steps.

This curious assemblage was ringed by modern walls, one of whose gateways was formed by the Arch of Hadrian where Turkish soldiers lounged, smoking their pipes in obvious indifference to the rare passers-by. The oriental aspect of the town never failed to strike new arrivals; this was indeed Turkey in Europe: men in turbans and flowing robes, occasionally a woman sheeted in white. Unless he was sufficiently familiar with the niceties of apparel in the Ottoman Empire to be able to distinguish Greek from Turk by the colour of their boots (the Greeks were seldom permitted the red and yellow ones) he would find recognisable natives only in the poorer inhabitants darting barefoot hither and thither in loose shirts tied at the waist, breeches to the knee and red skullcaps.

The best-known foreign resident was a French antiquarian and collector, Louis François Sebastien Fauvel, who had become an institution with a place all his own in the midst of the great monuments of the classical age: a Jupiter Guardian at the doorway of the vast museum that was Athens. He had started his career as an artist when in 1780 the Comte de Choiseul-Gouffier, requiring materials for a second volume of his *Voyage pittoresque de la Grèce*, engaged him to accompany the seasoned traveller Foucherot on a fact-finding expedition. So pleased was the Count with the results that when he was appointed French Ambassador to the Sublime

Porte at Constantinople, he invited Fauvel first to join the talented band that made up his artistic suite and then, in 1786, to take up residence in Athens as his representative.

Sir Richard Worsley was the lion of the town at that time, collecting a substantial booty of antiquities later published in his *Museum Worsleyanum*. More inhibiting to the debutant Fauvel, however, was the Turkish governor Hadji Ali Haseki, whose reign of terror lasted, with intermissions, till 1795. Under such ferocious despotism it was not easy to obtain antiquities, particularly as death could be the penalty for Turk or Greek if it was discovered that he had permitted any relics to be removed without the permission of the Sultan. Everything of that nature was considered to be crown property, though, as always in the Ottoman Empire, practice was often at variance with theory. In addition, the Count was apt to over-estimate the Sultan's influence on the situation in the outposts of the Empire such as Greece; no matter what promises to allow the removal of antiquities he might extract from the Sublime Porte, Fauvel could seldom obtain their implementation. 'Take everything you can,' he wrote in his often facetious vein, 'miss no occasion to pillage in Athens and the surrounding territory everything that is pillageable; spare neither the dead nor the living.'

So Fauvel devilled around the eastern Mediterranean for his patron; he explored, he identified forgotten sites and edifices, and he acquired what he could, where he could. In 1788, he stole an inscribed marble from the paved floor of a monastery for, he said, he could not obtain it in any other way; when he wished to remove three pieces of verd-antique columns that he had found forgotten in a corner of the Acropolis of Athens, he bribed a Turkish soldier to throw them from the walls of the citadel on to a dung-heap below. Then he set his sights on a Parthenon metope that a storm had brought down; it had been broken into three pieces by the fall, which in the event was fortunate, for otherwise it would have been impossible to induce the soldier, as he did, to slide the pieces along the walls above the theatre of Dionysos and drop them down to him below. When he unearthed a slab of the

Parthenon frieze, however, it was intact and, the Turks being particularly amenable to bribery, he obtained permission to remove it. But it proved too heavy and half the depth had to be sawn off the back, in which process the heads of the women sculptured on it in low relief were broken; they were not lost, however, for they accompanied the prize when he smuggled it down to the Piraeus for shipment. His booty was considerable: in 1787, he despatched to France for the Count sixteen cases of marbles and forty of plaster casts of the most important sculptures of Athens; the next year, over twenty more sculptured fragments took the same road.

Then came 1789 and the French Revolution. Fauvel's aristocratic patron took refuge in Russia; he remained in Greece, supporting himself by selling antiquities and lending the proceeds to the Athenians. He gladly acted as cicerone to the few travellers who called on him in his tiny study, formed from the upper story of the Monument of Lysicrates, then built into the walls of the hospitable Capuchin monastery. It was a different matter, however, when they tried to acquire antiquities. A young Englishman, Morritt of Rokeby in Yorkshire, negotiated with the Turkish commander of the Acropolis to hammer down the best of the Parthenon metopes, but Fauvel so frightened the Turk with the possibility of disciplinary action that he reneged on his promises to Morritt.

Another rival was that elegant English traveller John Hawkins, of Bignor Park in Sussex. However, he was in the habit of making his obode in an obscure village for a month or two, associating with the inhabitants and being led by them to every part of the country where they had observed any antiquities. He acquired a small collection that included a bronze figure of a Mercury, presented to him by a merchant of Jannina; it had been brought there from Paramythia about two years before, with other figures of equal beauty, by a person so ignorant of their value that he had disposed of them to a brazier; most had luckily been rescued by a Greek who had sold them in Russia.

In 1796, Fauvel was nominated a non-resident associate of the

Académie des Beaux-Arts and was well on the way to making his reputation as an antiquarian independently of his fugitive patron. But Napoleon invaded the Turkish dominion of Egypt and French nationals throughout the Ottoman Empire were imprisoned, Fauvel amongst them. When he was repatriated to France in 1801, he was ruined. He was nearly fifty years old and all his expertise concerned Greek antiquities. He had no place in Napoleon's France: world-famous works of art garnered throughout Europe as the spoils of victory were pouring into Paris: the Laocoon, the Belvedere Apollo, were on display in the Tuileries and it was such examples of Hellenistic art that were regarded as the most beautiful products of antiquity, for they had not yet been challenged by the Parthenon marbles. The sculptures and casts Fauvel had despatched to his patron evoked little interest when he was invited to place them on display in the Musée Napoléon; even the slab from the Parthenon frieze was left to lie disregarded in the reserves till Napoleon expressed astonishment that no work by Phidias, its supposed sculptor, was on view; it was hastily restored and exhibited and there it remained even when, in 1803, the Comte de Choiseul-Gouffier, having made his peace with Napoleon, was allowed to regain possession of all his antiquities except those built into the walls of the Museum: one of the Keepers hastily had it plastered in. The broken metope was, however, restored to the Count, then purchased by the Louvre after his death in 1818 for £1,250. The other metope Fauvel had acquired but left behind at Athens finished up in the British Museum.

None the less, Fauvel made valuable friends amongst the erudite of Paris. With their help he was nominated *Sous-commissaire* (vice-consul) at Athens and returned there early in 1803. But it was only to find that his quasi-monopoly of the antiquities had been broken. Collectors had invaded the land and were scouring it of its antiquities. Though he had a finger in almost every subsequent antiquarian pie, his pioneer days were over.

A number of circumstances had combined to focus artistic and acquisitive attention on Greece. War-torn Western Europe was closed to those inveterate travellers, the English, who could no longer pursue the Grand Tour through France and Italy; an alternative was the Ottoman Empire, slowly opening to western commerce and tourism, where the prestige of the English was rising as that of the French declined after Napoleon's invasion of Egypt. Furthermore, Italy had lost some of her attraction: the cream of her cultural heritage had been looted by the French; her antiquities had already been studied and published to satiety in the return to antiquity now known as neo-classicism; it was coming to be suspected that the true sources of European art were to be found in Greece and that Roman remains were derivative, if not decadent; it was feared that further excavations there would only swell the monotonous and serried ranks of routine imitations of the great Greek originals.

When the Earl of Elgin was appointed ambassador to the Sublime Porte in 1798, it is not surprising that he should have seen in his mission an opportunity to improve the taste of his country and contribute to progress in the fine arts and manufactures by procuring models of the best in Greek sculpture, architecture and decoration for the benefit of those who could not be privileged to see them *in situ*. We shall see what use his representatives made of the licence he was able to procure for them. Their acquisitions, however, were only a part of the plunder collected in Greece over the next thirty years by the travellers, artists and architects who profited from the outcrops of the past in the Ottoman Empire. Taking each classical site in turn, the history of its losses will be recounted in the following chapters.

2

THE ACROPOLIS OF ATHENS

A FORTRESS VILLAGE

The Acropolis was a Turkish fortress, commanded by a *disdar**
and garrisoned by troops described by Byron as the most ill-
regulated corps in the ill-regulated Ottoman Empire.

The path up to it lay through an Islamic cemetery from which
were visible the ruins of the theatre built for the Athenians by
their benefactor Herodes Atticus in the second century AD and
that had become an advance post of the fortress defences, linked
to them by bastions; its interior, 36ft deep in rubbish, was, like
that of the nearby theatre of Dionysos, sown in spring and
autumn with wheat, and the Turkish dervishes had erected on the
ruins of its proscenium a small shrine used for the administration
of the bowstring when a Turk was sentenced to death by strangu-
lation.

The citadel walls were, astoundingly, kept carefully covered
with a coat of whitewash, according to the usual Turkish mode of
concealing defects and inspiring respect from a distance. Certainly,
little enough was spent on repairing them or the buildings within:
buildings that had been shattered by exploding gunpowder,
damaged by bombardment, struck by lightning, looted, patched,
remodelled and built over to such an extent that it was a major
task to distinguish ancient Greek, Roman, medieval western, and
Turkish work in the confused jumble that amazed the artists and
architects who first climbed the fortress hill in modern times.

* A rank in the Turkish army, roughly equivalent to major.

21

The Propylaea—the monumental gateway—presented a most curious aspect. The central block had been damaged in 1687 when a Venetian bomb had ignited a powder magazine in it, blowing up the roof and doing dreadful damage to the façade. The spaces between its Doric columns had been walled up and a battery of guns raised on them, the capitals of the columns being knocked off for the purpose. The inner porch of the gateway was thus entirely masked, though Fauvel had been permitted by the Turks to inspect it and had seen several of the slender Ionic columns lying prostrate within; others had been broken up to buttress the fortifications.

The left-hand wing of the gateway had been transformed in medieval times to resemble nothing so much as a crusader's castle complete with battlements and slit windows, despite the damage done by a thunderbolt in 1699. As to the opposite wing, the whole Acropolis had been put to contribution by the Frankish dukes of Athens in the fourteenth century to raise a square tower, ninety feet high, on its foundations, part of the process of turning the Propylaea into a fortified residence. (The tower was demolished in 1875.)

But where was the little temple dedicated to Athene Nike? Seventeenth-century travellers had seen it standing on the bluff to the seaward side of the Acropolis, above the cliff from which Theseus' father had thrown himself on sighting the black sail of failure on the ship returning from Crete. The antiquarians of the early nineteenth century produced curious theories to account for its disappearance, even convincing themselves that their predecessors had seen a mirage and that the temple was buried under the Frankish tower. They finally realised that the Turks, faced in 1786 with an urgent need to strengthen the defences of the Acropolis against a rapidly advancing Venetian army, had completely demolished it, using the stones to construct a new rampart. Fortunately, the marble had not been harmed in the process and the little shrine was reassembled in 1835–6 (and again in 1936).

All this patching up and pulling down meant that the path into the citadel had to curve to the right around the base of the

Frankish tower, whose interior was used as a prison, to reach the back porch of the Propylaea. A Turkish dwelling had at one time been erected on it, but when lightning struck in 1645 the occupant and all his family perished in the ruins; the Turks had then used the remains as a powder magazine until lightning again made it a mark, in 1656, the resulting debris raising the level of the ground so high that it was barely possible to distinguish the tops of the exit doors.

The visitor could now turn towards the Parthenon—not as the ancient Athenians saw it, with its court of lesser temples and grove of votive statues, but hemmed in by a miserable Turkish village built from the ruins. The houses of the *disdar* and his lieutenant were the most solidly constructed and possessed gardens of moderate dimensions containing both flowers and vines, though these were hidden behind the high walls that concealed the women from sight. Most of the soldiers' huts were built of stones united only with mud and earth instead of mortar, so that their walls were continually falling and a heavy rain made nearly as much havoc as did a fire or an earthquake in other countries.

Finally standing before the Parthenon, the visitor would become aware of the dreadful damage suffered by this beautiful edifice. Lying along the line of their overthrow, disjointed pillars were piled on each other in the very sublimity of ruined art, proud even in their undeserved degradation; great gaps and fissures silently recalled the sculpture and decoration that once had filled them.

It was from a mortar battery sited on the nearby rise of the Areopagus that were fired the fatal shots that wrought the great destruction of 1687. The Venetian General Morosini's motley army was encamped round the rock; even though the Parthenon had been converted into a mosque, the Turks were using part of it as a temporary powder magazine and arsenal. One evening, at about 7 pm, two shells fired by a Hanoverian gunner chanced to land thereon and the whole exploded, destroying fourteen of the forty-six columns of the colonnade and most of the cella. (The north flank has since been rebuilt.) Debris even flew into the besiegers' camp. The Turks subsequently built themselves a small, shabby mosque within the remaining columns, where once the gold and ivory statue of Athene had received the veneration of her devotees. It stood askew, orientated towards Mecca, its white-washed walls, tiled roof and flat domes in ridiculous contrast to the noble symmetry around it. In the south-west corner angle, a minaret had been formed by adapting the bell tower that had been constructed in the Florentine taste by the Franks when the Parthenon had been their cathedral. The pavement was disfigured by a large opening made by the Turkish soldiers in order to use the foundations as an improvised quarry. (The interior of the Parthenon was cleared and the mosque demolished between 1835 and 1844.) Smoke from the neighbouring cottages had blackened the columns of the west front of the temple, that once had sparkled with the chaste and splendid brilliancy of its Pentelic marble; much of the rest was covered with the warm and mellow tint of an autumnal sunset, though to the south some parts nearly retained their original whiteness, whilst the northern side was in places shrouded in an almost imperceptible lichen of dusky green.

About half the original statues none the less remained in 1748, attested by a contemporary drawing, but by 1800 there were only four still in position. Two of them appeared to be of rather

Most of the statues that Phidias had placed in the pediments of the temple had disappeared. In the centre of the west gable, facing the Propylaea, had stood Athene and Poseidon contesting for the fair land of Attica, their chariot horses reined in behind them. In 1687, Morosini had decided that what remained of the group would form a suitable trophy of his ephemeral victory over the Turks. As one of Athene's horses was being lowered to the ground, the engineer's tackle broke and the sculpture crashed down, shattering into fragments. Other figures later followed suit, the worst indignity being suffered by the Poseidon which fell in such a way that the head was buried in the earth while the legs and the lower part of the body were exposed; the result was that the Turks broke off as much as could be seen and incrusted the fragments into the walls of the citadel.

About half the original statues none the less remained in 1748, attested by a contemporary drawing, but by 1800 there were only four still in position. Two of them appeared to be of rather whiter marble than their fellows, though in fact they had merely weathered less; this led many into the mistaken belief that they were Roman work, probably effigies of the Emperor Hadrian and his consort Sabina, erected in place of the original figures in gratitude for the Emperor's benefactions. The Sicilian traveller Scrofani expressed unbounded enthusiasm for the supposed Hadrian. 'Who could fail to recognise him,' Scrofani declaimed from his stance on a fragment of some fallen and shattered god, 'with his tranquil and serene air, his beard thick and curling, his noble and truly divine forehead? Who could this be but Hadrian, the friend of humanity, his statue almost intact? Why do only private persons come to Athens to admire it? If sovereigns came, they would see that time and the barbarians respect the image of virtuous monarchs.' Not only was the statue not Hadrian's, but he lost his head soon afterwards, as did his consort. In reality, they are original work and probably represent a river god and a nymph; the male head was presented to the English traveller Dodwell by a soldier of the Turkish guard; the female fell off of its own volition, or so the Turk who sold it to Fauvel said; both are now lost.

The east pediment had contained a representation of the birth of Athene. It was here that the first wound had been inflicted on the Parthenon: the early Christians, when converting the temple into a cathedral church, had built an apse into this front, taking down the centre group of the pedimental sculpture for the purpose, as if removing the principal actors from an antique tragedy, leaving only the chorus, seven of whom remained to either side of the gap. The east end had been the entrance to the Parthenon in antiquity, for it faced, of course, the rising sun, and it was there that the Panathenaic procession had halted, having wound its way up the hill, through the Propylaea and along the north flank of the temple. In the early nineteenth century, however, most scholars preferred to think that the entrance must have been to the west, facing the Propylaea, largely because they considered this to be the logical arrangement, quite regardless of the religious requirements of the Greeks. Examples are common at this time of a propensity to pronounce on the monuments of antiquity on the basis of an often garbled reading of an imperfect ancient text or even of personal prejudice.

The sculptured metopes that surrounded the temple above the outer columns, being so high, had suffered greatly from the elements, many being almost worn away. Morosini's explosion had brought down a large number, including sixteen of the best from the south flank. The frieze, representing the Panathenaic procession, that ran along the tops of the cella walls and over the inner columns of the porches had suffered not only from the explosion but from the Islamic hatred of representation of the living form that led the Turks to do so much wanton damage. Five slabs recorded in 1750 had disappeared, as had one on the east side moulded by Fauvel as recently as 1790.

The triple temple of the Erechtheion was in parlous condition. The maidens of the caryatid porch stood disgracefully mutilated, their faces besmeared with paint by Turkish fanaticism, their features chipped and broken. Whilst admiring the subtle variations in their attitudes, some travellers expressed doubt as to the propriety of representing the tender frame of a woman supporting the crushing weight of a marble roof; one had escaped her task nearly a hundred years before, perhaps to provide lime for the whitewash that covered the citadel buildings; a shabby rough wall was at times built up between them, closing the porch and hiding the steps, rediscovered by Fauvel, that led down into the main temple. Puzzled to explain the purpose of the porch, some antiquarians supposed it to have been constructed in that form to shelter Athene's legendary olive tree, conjured from the ground to win her contest with Poseidon; in fact, it had grown in the open ground of the sanctuary of Pandrosos immediately to the west of the Erechtheion, where a successor struggles today.

The rest of the Erechtheion was being gradually eroded: a piece of the architrave had been transported to the village of Ambelokoroi by a *disdar* and hollowed out to form a water trough for horses and cattle. A visitor, realising that its beautiful ornaments would soon be obliterated by the friction of the animals, offered the reigning *disdar* a considerable sum for the precious relic; but, notorious as was this Turk for his love of money, he refused to sell it, observing that it would be impious in him to take down what his father had erected.

Within the roofless walls of the main body of the Erechtheion could be viewed a confused jumble of stones and columns, a typical example of the difficulties confronting the antiquarian. The early Christians had disarranged all in converting it into a church, as Fauvel had been the first to discover; then it had been turned into a dwelling-house by the Frankish dukes; then the Turks had altered it for their residential purposes, abandoning it when it became too ruinous.

Finally, the noble north porch. Indifferent to the wrecking of the Propylaea and the Parthenon, the Turks had moved their gun-powder into this portico, constructing walls between its Ionic columns to enclose it; thus there wanted only a casual thunderbolt or the stupid negligence of a Turkish keeper to scatter in atoms this most exquisitely finished of all the Athenian edifices. The visitor could usually bribe a soldier to unbrick an entrance so that he might examine the intricately carved doorway between the porch and the temple, but a timber roof had been constructed by the Turks at the level of the top of this doorway, and to examine the makeshift upper chamber the visitor had to scramble along a plank to a breach in the outer wall. Once inside, however, he was amply rewarded, for he could inspect at leisure the beautiful coffers of the flat marble ceiling, examine the perfect volutes and delicate intertexture of wreaths and foliage of the Ionic capitals of the columns, and discover the small brass discs that decorated the eyes of the volutes and the beads of antique glass that had been fastened to the decorative banding in antiquity.

Near the Erechtheion was sited a gun battery commanding the town from which there ascended an amusing hum. The Turks used such artillery mainly to give warning of the commencement of the fast of Ramadan and on other public occasions; another twenty years would pass before it was fired in anger during the War of Independence.

ELGIN'S MISSION

It was not until Elgin reached Sicily in 1799, on his way to take up his post as envoy to the Sublime Porte, that recruitment for his artistic mission began. He followed ambassadorial precedent in first engaging a landscape artist, the Neapolitan Don Giovanni Battista Lusieri; but he broke new ground with the enlistment of a full supporting team of professional recorders and technicians: a figure artist, Theodore Iwanowitch, known as Lord Elgin's Calmuck from his origin in Central Asia, two architectural draughtsmen, and two *formatori* to make moulds of the sculpture and decoration from which plaster replicas would be cast.

When they arrived at Athens in August 1800, though they were at liberty to draw, measure and mould the monuments in the town, the Acropolis was intermittently closed to them. All Turkish strong-places were difficult of access—Navplion's Palamidi fortress was completely barred to foreigners—particularly when there was military activity in the Ottoman Empire such as the French invasion of Egypt. This was occasioned partly by fear of spies, partly in order to make a gesture of preparedness, however irrelevant, and partly because infidels battering at their gates in increasing numbers bored and distracted the Turks, who seized every excuse to revert to immobilism. For the Acropolis, there was the additional reason that the Franks,* when climbing over the ruins, necessarily overlooked the houses and gardens of the fortress village, obliging the inhabitants to confine their women out of sight. However, the *disdar* being of a particularly avaricious nature, cash payments or presents of coffee, tea and sugar usually ensured admission, the Turk receiving the pecuniary deposits somewhat in the manner of a turnpike man collecting a toll. A larger contribution was required for permission to make drawings and observations, as the young English architect Smirke discovered. He paid a fee of several pounds of coffee and

---

* Ever since French predominance in the Crusades, westerners of no matter what nationality had been called 'Franks' by the Levant peoples.

sugar, but afterwards the *disdar*, seeing him drawing, informed him that this could not be allowed for reasons of security. Having been advised by the English consul that this in fact meant another bribe, Smirke offered more coffee and sugar, only to be told that the *disdar* had enough of those articles and must have some other. In despair, the poor student bought and sent him a piece of silk costing nearly a guinea, but the *disdar* had the effrontery to send it back, saying that this was not enough and that Smirke should send him more of another colour, the pattern of which he enclosed.

Another Englishman, Dodwell, knowing that the *disdar* was a man of bad faith and insatiable rapacity, arranged for the English consul to conclude a bargain with the Turk for fifty shillings, in consideration of which Dodwell was to have access to the citadel as often as he chose, payment to take place only after all his drawings had been completed. Before long, however, the Turk became impatient and asked for part of the promised sum; upon refusal of this, he prohibited Dodwell's admission to the fortress. Dodwell, however, succeeded in gaining an entrance despite some insolent speeches from the soldiers and soon obtained their good graces by making small presents to their children; so accustomed did they become to this tribute that they would watch for their benefactor's arrival over the wall of the citadel, calling him 'the Frank of many paras'.* The *disdar* meanwhile becoming ever more impatient for the promised present, Dodwell frequently had his dinner sent up to the Acropolis in order to save time; the *disdar* seldom failed to drink most of the wine, observing that it was too good for studious people like artists. A ridiculous circumstance at length released the Englishman from these importunities. Engaged one day in drawing the Parthenon with the aid of a camera obscura,† he was asked by the *disdar* what new con-

* Forty paras made one silver Turkish piastre, worth about 3s 6d in 1800 but depreciated to about 5d by 1825. Gold Venetian sequins or Spanish dollars were universally accepted in lieu. All costs are specified in the English money of the time.

† The camera obscura is a dark box topped by an arrangement of mirror and lens, whereby the image of an object can be thrown on to a horizontal viewing floor; the outlines can then be drawn round the image.

juration was being performed by that machine and endeavoured to explain by making the Turk look into the camera; no sooner did the *disdar* see the temple reflected on the paper than he imagined Dodwell had produced the effect by some magical process; as he peeped into the camera again with a kind of cautious diffidence, some of his soldiers happened to pass and were beheld by the astonished Turk as if walking on the paper. He now became outraged, and after calling Dodwell pig and devil, told him that he might take away the whole temple but never again would he be permitted to conjure the soldiers into the box. When Dodwell found that it was in vain to reason with such ignorance, he changed his tone and stated that if the *disdar* did not cease his molestations, he would find himself put into the box and would find it very difficult to get out. The *disdar*'s alarm was visible; he never again made any difficulties.

Elgin's artists, his chaplain, the Reverend Philip Hunt, and even his parents-in-law, despite large bribes, were subjected to both arbitrary exclusion and gratuitous insult. Hunt reported these vexations and indignities to Elgin on his return to Constantinople, whilst stressing the value of the work none the less being accomplished by the mission. Having feasted one's eyes on the exquisite specimens of Athenian architecture, he said, every deviation from them, even the edifices of Rome itself, would almost disgust. Lusieri himself, though born on the banks of the Tiber, had become such an enthusiastic admirer of the Doric buildings of Greece that he shunned all evidences of Roman taste. Elgin determined to insist on a firman—a letter from the Sublime Porte—that would allow his mission to carry out their tasks unhampered.

The time was propitious, for the Sultan was bitterly resentful of the French invasion of Egypt, and the success of English arms in stopping them encouraged him to grant Elgin his every wish. The firman issued on 6 July 1801 was entirely satisfactory: it accorded permission to the artists to enter the Acropolis in order to draw, measure and model with plaster the monuments there, to erect scaffolding for the purpose, to excavate the ancient foundations and to search for inscriptions. It also—a provision that was to prove even more significant—commanded that no obstacles should be placed in the way of the mission taking away pieces of stone with inscriptions and figures.

Now came the more difficult part of the transaction, ensuring the implementation of the firman. Choiseul-Gouffier had had little success: Elgin was to do better. Chaplain Hunt, temporarily become a diplomat, was about to embark on a progress around the pashaliks of western Turkey and was chosen to present the firman in Athens. He arrived accompanied by a representative of the Sultan as well as an impressive retinue of underlings to pay a ceremonial visit to the Governor.* Speaking in a most determined tone, he insisted that the provisions of the firman be carried out. The Governor, aware of Elgin's standing at Constantinople, became quite submissive and expressed his mortification that the *disdar* should have treated any Englishman with disrespect or demanded money on any pretext. Hunt was resolved, however, to see the *disdar*'s son, the chief culprit, brought before the Governor so that the blame could be laid fairly and squarely on his shoulders. When the miscreant came in barefoot and trembling, he attempted to deny the facts, but on Hunt's repeating his accusations, the Governor told the wretch he was to be exiled. Hunt then interceded for him, on promise of future good conduct, and he was pardoned, though it was hinted that he might well find employment in the Sultan's galleys on a second complaint. The conference ended with renewed assurances that henceforward the citadel would be open to all Englishmen from sunrise to sunset to draw, measure and model and that Elgin's mission might carry away whatever did not interfere with the defences of the citadel.

Hunt did not rely on these assurances without the backing of a judicious selection of appropriate presents. Telescopes, watches, crystal bottles, chandeliers, horses, guns, Wedgwood pottery,

---

* The Governor, or *Voivode*, was the superior of the *disdar* and of the *Cadi* or Chief Justice; he was Chief of Police and tax-gatherer, having bought this right from the Sublime Porte for upwards of £7,500, and sought to make as large a profit as possible. The old *disdar* died about this time; as he and his son were equally avaricious, no distinction is made between them in the text.

cloaks and narghiles were showered on the Turks from now on. Even so, no time was lost in case the Turks should change their minds: all available masons and porters were rounded up and set to search the Acropolis for antiquities.

At this point, a distinction must be made between, on the one hand, the sculpture still remaining on the buildings and, on the other, the fallen and often buried fragments.

The ambitions of Hunt and Lusieri soon rose above the latter: they coveted the better specimens that, though sadly damaged, tempted them from the walls. Armed with the bait of English gold and manufactures, Hunt induced the Governor to accord an authorisation to remove the least damaged of the metopes still adorning the Parthenon. On 31 July 1801, the carpenter of a ship lying in the harbour, aided by five of the crew and twenty Greeks, scaled the walls of the edifice and, using windlasses and cords from the ship, unslotted and lifted the best of the metopes and lowered it without the slightest accident. Next day, another metope was removed. When Hunt saw the beautiful marble hanging in the air and depending on Mediterranean cordage, he was seized with a trembling and palpitation that ceased only when it safely reached the ground.

From then on, there was nothing to stop removals wholesale, with the sculpture *in situ* regarded as legitimate prey. Before leaving Athens, Hunt made it very clear to the Governor that hearty compliance was expected with the spirit of the Porte's instructions, as regards both the artists' freedom to work and the removal of any of the sculpture that interested Elgin.

It was, however, after Hunt's departure that there took place the 'extraordinary excess' viewed with inexpressible mortification by three English travellers, the tutor Clarke and his pupil Cripps, and Dodwell.

To understand what happened, it is necessary first to look at the construction of the Parthenon. When the outer row of fluted columns had been set in position, a marble beam, the architrave, had been placed on them; above this had been raised a decorative band about four feet high consisting of a series of panels, alter-

Page 33 (*above*) The French consul, Fauvel, being served by his house-keeper on the balcony of his Athens house; (*below left*) C. R. Cockerell from a drawing by Ingres; (*below right*) Jakob Linckh by Vogelstein

Page 34 (left) C. von Haller by Cockerell; (below) the west front of the Propylaea at Athens. Bastion constructed from the remains of the Temple of Athene is on the left and Frankish tower used as a prison on the right. The Turkish governor is in the centre of the group in the foreground

nately triglyphs decorated with vertical bands and grooves, and metopes sculptured in high relief; the metope panels had been slotted in between the triglyphs so that when the cornice was set above them, they were sealed into place by it. As a result of the Morosini explosion, it was comparatively easy to unslot and remove many of the surviving metopes, but at the south-east angle there remained several in a fine state of preservation still sealed in place by the cornice above.

One day, while Dodwell was sketching on the Acropolis, Clarke and Cripps were paying a visit conducted by Lusieri, who had become a good friend of theirs. Some Greek workmen, under the latter's direction, were engaged in making preparation, by means of ropes and pulleys, for taking down these particular metopes. After a short time spent in examining the several parts of this extremity of the temple, a labourer informed Lusieri that one of the metopes was about to be lowered. It was raised from its station between the triglyphs; but, the workmen endeavouring to give it a position adapted to the projected line of descent, a part of the adjoining masonry was loosened by the machinery and down came the fine masses of Pentelic marble, scattering their white fragments with thundering noise among the ruins. The *disdar* himself had come to view the work; seeing this, he could no longer restrain his emotion, but actually took his pipe from his mouth and, letting fall a tear, said in the most emphatic tone of voice, 'Telos' (No more), positively declaring that nothing would induce him to consent to any further dilapidation of the building.

According to Lusieri's later version of this incident, the *disdar*'s tearful words signified only his regret that this was the last of the metopes it was intended to detach and therefore the last for which he would receive his usual payment in advance. It was not, however, the last, nor did the *disdar*'s resolution persist in the face of the presents with which Lusieri was enabled, through the munificence of Elgin, to tempt his avariciousness. In the end, almost the whole of what had remained of the cornice on the south side, as well as the south-eastern angle of the pediment, was thrown down and utterly broken.

Further damage was done when Lusieri came to remove a number of the slabs of the frieze from the cella walls. The men employed laboured long and ineffectually with iron crowbars to move the stone of the firm-built walls; when they succeeded, each slab as it fell shook the ground with its ponderous weight, with a deep hollow noise; it seemed like a convulsive groan from the injured spirit of the temple.

Prominent amongst the early removals were the statues from the Parthenon pediments. Disdaining the supposedly Roman figures on the west front, Hunt and Lusieri appropriated the two others still in position; from the east gable, they removed all the extant statues as well as the head of the Moon Goddess's horse.

Next to receive attention was the Erechtheion. Hunt suggested removing the entire caryatid porch, which project Elgin supported with enthusiasm; Napoleon, he said, had got nothing comparable from his Italian sweep. But practical difficulties precluded such an ambitious undertaking, as they did Hunt's designs on the Monument of Lysicrates in Athens town and the Lion Gate at Mycenae. Finally, Lusieri took only the best-preserved of the caryatids, a brick pillar being set in her place; he also removed the capital from the southern anta of the body of the temple and one of the Ionic columns of the portico. For Elgin, true to his aim of improving the taste of his country, wished to have, in the actual object, a complete set of each type of architectural ornament, each cornice, each frieze, each decorated ceiling, as well as specimens of the capitals and columns of each of the different architectural orders, Doric, Ionic, and Corinthian, and of their variant forms: a staggering order, given the vast variety of Greek architecture and decoration, that Lusieri could only very partially fulfil.

Who should be regarded as responsible for removing the sculpture still in position? The initiative was Hunt's, and he was the moving spirit in the first major removals, with Lusieri first seconding and then taking over from him; such action was, however, in line with Elgin's known wishes, and though the original intention had been only to draw, measure and mould the antiquities, Elgin endorsed his representatives' operations and enthusiastically urged their prosecution at the Parthenon and elsewhere.

Who should be blamed for the damage involved in the execution? Clarke attempted to throw the onus on Elgin, whom he greatly disliked, and to exculpate his friend Lusieri on the grounds that the artist could only obey the orders he received and did so with manifest reluctance. But Lusieri paid no heed to any remonstrances, whether from the *disdar* or from visiting Englishmen, continuing his dilapidations with no apparent distaste. Dodwell's view was that the matter would never have been carried to the extraordinary excess of the destruction of the cornice had Elgin been present at the time; the management of the whole affair, he maintained, had been committed to the hands of mercenary and interested persons and executed with all the unprincipled licentiousness of subordinate and hireling agents. For Elgin did not himself visit Greece until nine months after the first removals, in the spring of 1802, and cannot have been aware until after the event of the damage involved.

The justification later put forward for the removals was, in the first place, that if the English had not acted, the French would have. True, Fauvel had attempted to obtain specimens, but his efforts had remained largely ineffectual. True also that the *disdar* told Hunt that Fauvel had paid £50 for permission to remove a metope but that, as it was being taken down, the rope had broken and it had been dashed to a thousand pieces and that Hunt appears to have believed this mendacious ruse to induce him to increase his tribute (for Fauvel's acquisitions, cf Chapter 1). True finally that French competition may have been feared when it was thought that Napoleon, foiled in Egypt, might attempt to force a way to the East via Greece. But in 1801, the French were under anathema at the Porte and Elgin's expressed fear of their rivalry came only later when they had made peace with the Sultan and it could be used as a goad to energise Lusieri into obtaining and shipping every available antiquity. Lusieri's contention that Elgin decided to remove the sculpture only when he heard that

French agents were negotiating to strip the Acropolis is un-
acceptable.

A more valid justification was the fact that under Muslim
oppression, for which no relief then appeared foreseeable, the
sculptures had been most distressingly exposed to wilful damage
and that the Turks had been eager to break off whatever they could
reach, not only through fanaticism but in hopes of disposing of
such fragments to the Franks. Though the flood of predatory
visitors had barely started at the time of Elgin's mission, enough
has been said of previous damage to support this contention. Had
the Turks carried out their threat during the War of Independence
to destroy the Acropolis buildings, Elgin would have been hailed
as the saviour of the sculptures.

Turning now to the removal of the fallen sculpture, there can
be no doubt as to the debt owed to Elgin's mission: many such
fragments would have continued to furnish the lime-kilns of the
Turks whilst others would have been appropriated by visitors to
finish up scattered in museums throughout Europe or be lost
when their owners lost interest in them. Several of the marbles in
the British Museum owe their survival to chance, like the sepulchral monument recorded in Athens in 1720 that disappeared
until dug up below a house in New Bond Street some 150 years
later.

One area of the Acropolis was expected to yield a particularly
rich harvest: that in front of the west pediment, where Morosini's
engineer had let the sculpture crash to ruin. Sure enough, when
the cottage of one of the Turkish garrison had been bought and
pulled down, numerous fragments were retrieved, including the
torso of Iris, whose diaphanous drapery had miraculously with-
stood her brutal handling. Great efforts were then made to purchase another hut nearby, but the owner made every kind of
difficulty and extorted a high price; when his dwelling was demolished, neither it nor the ground it was built on yielded one
piece of marble; its former owner then laughingly announced
that he had burnt all the fragments he could find to make lime for
the mortar used in constructing his vanished home.

The Turks refused the mission nothing, even going so far as to allow sculptured marbles that had been built into the Acropolis fortifications to be removed: four sadly damaged slabs of the frieze of the demolished temple of Athene Nike were extracted from the bastion that had been constructed from its stones, and the centre slab from the east side of the Parthenon frieze was prised out of the citadel wall. The latter was found too cumbersome to be transported conveniently, so Lusieri decided to have part of the back sawn off to lighten it; this was not well done, for want of sufficiently fine saws, and it parted in the middle during its progress down the hill, fortunately at a place where there was no sculpture. A gun carriage and a train of thirty men were at times barely sufficient to transport the finds. They were first taken to the house of the English consul to be drawn by Lord Elgin's Calmuck, then crated and dragged to the Piraeus to await shipment.

At the outset, none of the protagonists appears to have felt any qualms over the removals. It must not be forgotten that a general atmosphere of pillage then prevailed, with Napoleon transporting his cultural loot to Paris, the new Rome; why should London not become the new Athens? However, they were soon to be surprised and disquieted by the condemnations of English travellers, culminating in the denunciations of Byron. Hunt soon realised that there were envious people who would not fail to represent what had been done as a violence to the fine remains of Greek sculpture, and when he later gave evidence before the parliamentary committee considering the purchase of the Elgin marbles, he implied that he had been responsible for taking down only one metope, unjustifiably shouldering the onus for the other removals on to Elgin. For his part, Lusieri announced his intention of devoting himself to executing in Athens the best paintings of his life so that some barbarisms he had been obliged to commit in his patron's service might be forgotten.

What did the Greeks think of all these removals? Hunt later testified that there was no resentment in Athens in any class, the common inhabitants being always ready to act as labourers in removing the sculptures; Elgin's secretary Hamilton shared this view, adding that the Athenians regarded such activities as a means of bringing foreigners into the country and of having money spent amongst them. Neither Turks nor Greeks seem, in reality, to have been quite so indifferent. Lusieri told Clarke that the Turks did not like the removal of the sculpture from the Parthenon since they regarded the temple with religious veneration, it having been for so long a mosque. There had also been murmurs when Hunt asked for the Erechtheion porch, for the Athenians were extremely attached to it and Lusieri did not think removal possible without a special firman. According to Dodwell, the Athenians lamented the ruin that was committed and loudly and openly blamed their Turkish overlord for the permission he had granted.

Superstition played a significant role here. A curious notion prevailed amongst the people regarding ancient statues: they believed that these were real bodies, mutilated and exchanged into their present state of petrification by magicians who would have power over them as long as the Turks were masters of Greece; if the country became independent, they would be transformed into their former bodies; the spirit within them was called an *Arabim* and was not infrequently heard to moan and bewail its condition. It was said that some Greeks carrying a chest of Elgin marbles to the Piraeus threw it down and could not for some time be prevailed upon to touch it again, affirming that they heard the *Arabim* crying out and groaning for his fellow-spirits detained in bondage on the Acropolis; they supposed that the condition of these enchanted marbles would be bettered by a removal from the country of the tyrant Turks. A quite different belief co-existed happily, for the Erechtheion caryatids were reported to have emitted great nocturnal lamentations for their sister taken by Lusieri, and when Lord Guildford later supplied a copy to replace her, the Athenians would have it that this was the original maiden who, refusing to stand erect in England, had necessarily been returned to her Grecian birthplace. When a column of the temple of Olympian Zeus was destroyed, the others were heard at night to lament the loss, and these plaints did not cease to terrify the inhabitants till the governor responsible for the sacrilege was himself destroyed by poison after appointment to another post.

As to the antiquarian passion of the *Milordi* in general, their restless activity, their excavations, measuring and drawing, the Greeks regarded this with considerable reprobation or, more charitably, with a kind of compassion, thinking it to be a form of madness or else the feverish curiosity of he who runs about to find something to do because he has no legitimate pursuits to which to devote his attention. The inquisitive traveller who was neither a merchant nor a doctor and who spent his money without getting anything in return—or, at least, anything considered to be of value—was almost as incomprehensible to them as to the Turks. When the Governor of Corinth heard that two Englishmen were collecting fragments of pottery scattered amongst the ruins of the ancient city, he sent for them and inquired rather sharply who they were. 'English gentlemen,' was the answer. 'Gentlemen?' he repeated, 'and is it like gentlemen to be seen picking up pieces of broken pots and groping among heaps of rubbish?' There was so much apparent reason in this remark and it was so utterly impossible to explain to a Turk the real nature or object of such a search, that the Englishmen thought it best to let him have his opinion and, passing quietly for paupers beneath his notice, make an obeisance and retire.

As time went by, however, antiquarian research came to be tolerated and even encouraged, because it was supposed to be tacitly agreed that the *Milordi* would pay double for everything. This seemed only fair to the inhabitants of some of the remoter districts, who believed that the English frequently found treasures, the coins from which they changed into flies that winged their way to the West where they reverted to their former metallic form. In the towns, however, it was believed that if the English obtained an antique they could sell it in their own country at a price sufficient to pay for their whole Levant tour—a shrewd estimation. It was even thought that the English travelled so much because their own country was too expensive for them to live in.

THE FRANCO-BRITISH ANTIQUITIES WAR, 1803–12

'How are the mighty fallen, when two painters contest the privilege of plundering the Parthenon and triumph in turn, according to the tenor of each succeeding firman,' wrote Byron.

The English party committed the first act of aggression in the antiquities war: whilst Fauvel was absent (1799–1803) they were permitted by the Turks to appropriate his tools, blocks and tackle, and cart, the only cart in Athens, brought all the way from Toulon. Worse still, they attempted to seize or buy the twenty-three cases of antiquities and loose marbles that he had been obliged to leave stored at the Capuchin monastery when he was arrested; Lusieri was staying at the monastery and they must have presented a standing temptation. The attempt failed, however.

In return, the French party could use only guerrilla tactics such as suborning the loyalty of Elgin's artists. Lusieri's suspicions were soon aroused, however, and he watched his charges strictly to prevent them smuggling drawings and measurements to the enemy. It must have been a distracting and distasteful task, and he complained that the artists had no manners, no culture, no religion, and far too high an opinion of themselves; the Calmuck, in particular, was incorrigibly lazy, much too fond of the bottle and of a flighty mind.

All this amounted to mere skirmishing until, in February 1803, Elgin relinquished his post as ambassador to the Sublime Porte and sailed for home via Athens, picking up all the artists except Lusieri, who was left to complete the tasks of the mission. Travelling overland from Italy, however, Elgin was made a prisoner of war by Napoleon and his influence was eclipsed. Meanwhile, Fauvel had returned to Athens as French vice-consul and the antiquities war could begin in earnest, for the balance of power was altering in Constantinople, as it always did if patience was exercised, and the French were returning to favour. Fauvel began by drawing up a strong protest against Lusieri's activities, but it was delayed *en route* to Constantinople and it was not till early in 1804 that he was able to tell the *disdar* that he had received instructions from his ambassador to make a list of everything that Elgin had acquired from the Acropolis for despatch to the capital; the Turk was so frightened that he forbade any more removals by Lusieri. The French ambassador, whilst feeling that it would be only proper to wait awhile after his protestations against Elgin's operations, was prepared to undertake some excavations at his own expense under the direction of Fauvel; but the delay was fatal and the plan died of inanition.

Lusieri had meanwhile made enemies amongst the Athens visitors: Dodwell (who condemned him as responsible for the damage to the Parthenon), Gell and Sir Charles Monck. According to Lusieri, the two latter attempted to undertake diggings without obtaining firmans or asking permission from the Governor or from the owner of the land, or being willing to pay anything; the Governor stopped them, telling all that he would allow no one to dig but Lusieri. When, therefore, a new governor was appointed in 1805, Gell's hints that Lusieri was no longer supported by the English embassy in Constantinople soon reached his ears; finding himself accused, in addition, of having accepted huge bribes to permit Elgin's activities (of which he had, of course, known nothing) his solution was to place a total ban on all excavations in Athens and the surrounding countryside.

Next year, Fauvel returned to the charge, beseeching the new French ambassador to obtain a firman for him; he was unsuccessful. Then Pouqueville, the French consul at the court of Ali Pasha of Jannina, offered to procure an authorisation to excavate in that despot's domains; the necessary funds were not forthcoming from the ministry in Paris.

Fauvel's real opportunity came in 1807, when Russia, supported by England, declared war on Turkey. Now he could pay the English back in their own coin and seize their antiquities awaiting shipment. He enlisted the help of his friend Pouqueville; Ali Pasha, being in an anti-English phase, was ready to co-operate; just as Lusieri, fearing for his personal safety as well as for that of his collections, was preparing to leave Athens with the most portable of the antiquities, Ali's emissary, accompanied by local officials, presented himself at the artist's house, stating that by his master's orders all antiquities assembled there were to be sequestrated. Everything was sealed up, but Lusieri managed to escape, penniless and in poor health; he eventually found refuge in Malta and then in Sicily.

None the less, Fauvel failed to obtain possession of Lusieri's marbles. The impetuous Pouqueville was over-optimistic when he jubilantly asserted that all Elgin's prospects of removing the rest of his antiquities were now checkmated, that they would be sent to Paris, and that if the English party in Athens ventured to protest, Ali would soon shut them up. English command of the Mediterranean precluded movement by sea, and the Pasha's muleteers pronounced it impossible to move the unwieldy marbles over the mountain tracks to the west coast; all that could be appropriated was Lusieri's collection of vases. Ali sent the best of them off as a present to Napoleon but his messenger abandoned them on learning that he would have to go to Vilna to find the Emperor; the English consul Leake benefited from the remainder. The cases of marbles remained intact at Athens.

The antiquities war was being waged at sea as well as on land, for it was not enough to cull the marbles and painted vases; they had also to be shipped. One of the curious aspects of the naval situation in the Mediterranean was the possibility for personages like Elgin to use HM ships for the transport of their acquisitions. English captains were free to give passage to any person they chose, even in wartime; it seems that heavy marbles could be regarded as being in the same category. At first, no great export difficulty was experienced by Elgin's mission, who early on had a real stroke of fortune when HMS *Braakel*, commanded by the brother of tutor Clarke, ran aground at the Piraeus. Hunt was in Athens and was able materially to assist in saving the ship, enlisting the help of the Governor and some 100 Athenians; the Governor drew the ship's horoscope, from the result of which, he assured everyone, there was no doubt she would be saved; the

Athenians lightened her and warped her off the rocks. In gratitude for Hunt's help, Captain Clarke was disposed to take on board everything that was ready for shipment: forty-four of the heaviest cases were soon in the holds of his ship.

Fauvel was not so fortunate with the twenty-four cases of antiquities he had long before gathered for Choiseul-Gouffier. Reconciled to his former patron, he handed them over for shipment in the French frigate *l'Arabe* in 1803; this vessel fell a prey to the English navy and the antiquities were seized as spoils of war.*

Elgin also encountered disaster at sea. His own ship, the *Mentor*, loaded with a cargo that included pieces of the Parthenon frieze, was wrecked off the island of Cerigo; the marbles were recovered only with the greatest difficulty, and even then Elgin had to enlist the help of Nelson in getting them shipped to Malta in convoy.

After Lusieri's return to Athens in 1810, there still remained some forty cases of Elgin's antiquities at the Piraeus; the Turks refused permission to move them without a firman from Constantinople, contending that Elgin had never had permission to take the sculptures and could hardly expect a licence to export them now. Elgin even considered mounting an armed raid to seize them by main force. Prudent counsels prevailed, however, not least those of Lusieri, even though his first attempt to ship them was foiled: when he chartered and loaded a Hydriote boat, the Turks made him unload everything, to the delight of the anti-Elgin faction. But English stock was rising again at the Sublime Porte: the new ambassador obtained the necessary firman and most of the cases were despatched despite the vigorous protests of Fauvel. Another five were shipped in 1811 to Malta in company with Lusieri and Byron, while still more left with Captain Percival the same autumn.

With these shipments, the antiquities war petered out. The two

---

* They included a Parthenon metope. Three years later, Elgin's agents bought them for £1 a case at a London customs house clearance sale, assuming them to be his. When he discovered the mistake, he offered to return the metope at least to the count, but war conditions and misunderstandings prevented restitution.

artists, older and wiser, settled down to enjoy their beloved Athens without further contention. An Englishman reports that when he was walking with Lusieri in 1812 they met Fauvel, who turned to accompany them.

The negotiations for the sale of Elgin's marbles to the nation were not concluded till 1816. Controversy over their artistic worth had erupted almost as soon as the first consignment was uncrated. To connoisseurs and artists accustomed to the grace and elegance displayed by the statues they had seen, drawn and procured in Italy, the strong spirit of the Grecian marbles came as a shock. Some, like the collector R. P. Knight, put their heads in the sand and condemned the pedimental sculpture as botched Roman work and the metopes and frieze as the product of artisans carving rough decoration intended to be viewed at a distance. Weighty opinions, however, were ranged in the opposite camp, not least those of Visconti, Keeper of Antiquities at the Louvre, the sculptor Canova and the collector Prince Ludwig of Bavaria. Finally, on the recommendation of the Parliamentary Select Committee set up to examine the question, they were purchased for £35,000, a figure that was far from covering Elgin's costs in presents, transport, retrieval of shipwrecked cargo, interest etc estimated by him at £62,440.

CONTINUING DEPREDATION AND DAMAGE

The bans imposed in the antiquities war did not save the Acropolis from continuing dilapidation.

The Turks carried on much as before: the Propylaea lost the remaining part of the cornice of its front porch, taken down to provide a coffin for the deceased wife of a Turkish dignitary; the Erechtheion was deprived of another section to strengthen the fortifications.

The visitors who flocked to the citadel also took their toll. The young architect Smirke looked about among the heaps of ruins and found a fragment of an enriched moulding that he coveted greatly. Unfortunately, there was a large piece of marble attached to it that made it difficult to carry without his being seen by the guards at the entrance to the citadel. A friend visited the citadel with him one morning; they carried the fragment between them to the side of one of the fortress walls and hurled it over; when it reached the ground, it unfortunately dashed along for a considerable distance, only stopping at length on the road which wound up to the entrance. They hurried down, wrapped their handkerchieves over it, and brought it safely to their lodgings.

Another English architect, Inwood, later followed this example. He had obtained permission from the *disdar* to detach and remove various fragments, including a piece of coffered ceiling and a part of one of the Ionic capitals from the demolished temple of Athene Nike; but soon afterwards he found a fragment of a Corinthian capital and, fearing a rebuff if he attempted openly to remove this additional item, he rolled it down the rock on the north side to a person waiting there to receive it. It was, not surprisingly, somewhat injured in the process.

Yet another architect, Cockerell, acquired a portion of the Parthenon frieze in a similar manner. The *disdar* had become exceedingly attached to him, and when Cockerell went to pay a farewell visit, the Turk announced that he would make him a present. Knowing that his young friend was fond of old sculptured stones, the *disdar* invited him to bring a cart to the base of the Acropolis at a certain hour at night so that he could be given something, adding that it could not be done in the daytime for fear of giving offence to the Greeks. Cockerell kept the appointment: as he drew near there was a shout from above to look out and without further warning a block of the frieze was bowled down the cliff. Such treatment of it had not been anticipated by the astonished recipient, but it was too late for regrets; it was put on to the cart, shipped to England and presented to the British Museum.*

As increasing numbers of Frankish ships put into the Piraeus, the Acropolis came into grave jeopardy, for the petty officers and ratings of both merchant ships and vessels of war had a great

* Right-hand half, end slab, South frieze at BM.

propensity to break off pieces as memorials; though thousands of fragments still lay about, nothing apparently satisfied them unless they performed their share of direct mutilation. The caryatid porch of the Erechtheion encountered the greatest peril. Authorship of a note supposed to have been picked up near the Piraeus was attributed by Athenian scandal to an English midshipman; it read as follows:

> I have lost the ear that I took away from one of those stone women on the top of the hill; Smith has got the other; so, as I don't like his having a prize which I have lost, will you have the goodness, as you are going there tomorrow, to chip me off the nose neatly and let me have it before we sail.

The text may be apocryphal, but the traveller Laurent affirms that he actually saw the vandal deed being perpetrated. Visiting the Acropolis one day, he came upon a midshipman standing on the base of one of the caryatids, clinging with his left arm round the lady, while his right hand, provided with a hard and heavy pebble, was endeavouring to knock off the only remaining nose of those beautifully sculptured statues. Laurent exerted his eloquence in vain to preserve this monument of art from the juvenile Alaric.

It was not unusual before long to see a party of men-of-war's stewards, with a lady's maid, scrambling over the fallen stones with a picnic basket. An eye-witness recounts that, as one of them busied himself in spreading their repast of cold meat, warm wine and porter, another gallantly offered a pencil to the lady; pointing to the cornice of the caryatid porch, he said: 'There is a nice place to write your name.' 'Well, I declare, that's lucky,' she replied, 'I thought we should not have found room anywhere.'

Indeed, a dozen or more names aiming at posterity, all together in a scroll, often denoted an irruption from some ship in the offing. Sailors were far from being the only offenders, however: Elgin and his wife carved their names half-way up one of the Parthenon columns: though his was soon obliterated, hers was still visible years later. On one of the caryatids could be descried the words 'Opus Pheidiae' and, on the pillar substituted for the maiden removed by Lusieri, 'Opus Elgin'.

Many writers inveighed against the practice of name-carving which, however much derided, had led the most eminent travellers, in common with the most insignificant, to leave their names in some conspicuous situation. The vast number of those who were thus emulous, it was said, must prove fatal to antiquity; if they did not weaken the column they inscribed and hasten its decay, they drew away the mind from the contemplation of other times to anathematise the folly of modern ones. One might as well look upon an ancient marble enveloped in modern cement as observe a Doric column covered with names, of which a great portion were little honour to their owners and could not be more so to the column itself.

It is not known how some of the Parthenon fragments that adorned the collections of Europe were obtained: the sale of Vivant Denon's antiquities in 1819 included a female foot that had inexplicably come from one of the west metopes of the Parthenon; pieces have been identified in the museums of Karlsruhe, Padua, Palermo and the Vatican, and one was even dug up in a garden in Essex in 1902. A few fragments have been assigned to their captors, like the centaur's head acquired in 1812 by the Bavarian Martin Wagner, now in the museum of the University of Würzburg. It is to be feared that many others were simply lost.

Depredation and damage were fortunately not the only activities of visitors. Architects and artists were constantly studying the edifices, from the little society we shall meet in Chapters 6 and 7 to the intrepid Vulliamy who was accustomed to stand on the crumbling ruins of the Parthenon to measure as tranquilly as if he had been on terra firma.

Hobhouse had written in 1812: 'I have said nothing of the possibility of the ruins of Athens being, in the event of a revolution in favour of the Greeks, restored and put into a condition capable of resisting the ravages of decay; for an event of that nature cannot, it strikes me, have ever entered into the head of any one who has seen Athens and the modern Athenians.' He was to be proved wrong.

3

ATHENS AND ATTICA

THE TOWN OF ATHENS

The reader will have remarked the parallel between the careers of
Lusieri and Fauvel. Both artists, both chosen by an ambassador as
artistic representative at Athens, both required to collect antiquities, a task for which they had been in no way prepared; both
evicted from Athens as a result of conflicts between the Great
Powers and forced to leave their acquisitions behind them; both
trying to seize each other's collections and failing. In addition,
they both delighted to act as cicerone to the visitors, mostly
English, who came to their adopted city.

Many a returning traveller mentioned 'Don Tita', as Lusieri
was known, often with affection; his meagre figure sitting at an
easel under the shade of a large umbrella, a white beaver hat with
a black cockade on his head, was a familiar sight. Hamilton,
during all his travels for Elgin, never met anyone to whom he
felt really attached as a friend except Lusieri; but he warned a
later visitor, Cockerell, that Lusieri could be touchy, and Cockerell
found indeed that the artist required a good deal of courting.

Fauvel was more approachable. He never appeared his age
despite years passed in the debilitating climates of the Levant, nor
did his caustic wit lose its bite, even if some visitors found that he
claimed to have pioneered any and every discovery. When he took
his callers to view the town, he was accompanied also by his two
spaniels who could almost have acted as guides themselves, for
they stopped of their own accord at the points where their master

Page 51 (*above*) Athens, the Acropolis. The Parthenon with mosque within is on the right and the Erechtheion on the left; (*below*) Erechtheion, showing caryatid porch

Page 52 (*above*) Athens: Capuchin Monastery, showing the Monument of Lysicrates; (*below*) festival around the Theseion

was in the habit of delivering his learned commentaries. A little
procession would soon form: the janissary* and curious children
would walk in front, pausing when they came to one of the
carvings, cornices or capitals that served as milestones, doorposts
or paving stones; looking back, they would try to guess from
Fauvel's expression whether it was in good taste; if the consul
shook his head, they would shake theirs too and go to stand four
paces farther on in front of another morsel.

The custom of inserting sculptured and inscribed stones over
the doorways of houses turned the lanes of Athens into a veritable
gallery of marbles. The Greeks regarded such fragments as charms
to guard their dwellings; nevertheless, some travellers, thrown
into a frenzy of acquisitiveness at the sight of so many apparent
treasures so carelessly disposed, succeeded in inducing the owners
to part with them. The fragments were for the most part worth-
less, and after adorning the courtyards of the houses rented by the
Milordi, were often left behind as useless and untransportable
lumber.

Inwood bargained for one such fragment and, as soon as a
price of ten shillings had been agreed, the master of the house
took a small axe and prised the morsel out. A Greek widow who
lived opposite promptly appeared in her doorway and, pointing to
the fragment over it, inquired if the gentleman would purchase
that also. An offer was made of a further ten shillings; that, the
Greek matron replied, was not in a fair ratio, for her fragment
was twice the size of that on the opposite side of the way and
ought therefore to be worth £1. At this a general laugh followed
amongst the neighbours who had assembled and the young
gentleman was not permitted to depart without adding her piece to
his purchase. Still not content, Inwood discovered, in a ruined
chapel near the Ilyssos, a damaged fragment of an Ionic capital
built into an interior wall. A Greek offered to remove it for him,
making out that this could be done only secretly at night, since
otherwise the Turks might seize it to offer it for sale at an exorbi-

* A janissary was a Turkish soldier hired from a pasha or local military commander
and paid about 5s a day.

tant price, or the monks might claim it as the property of the monastery to which the building might originally have belonged. Inwood struck a bargain with the Greek, but the rascal, instead of bringing him the morsel, took it to his own house and refused to deliver it without much additional entreaty and, one suspects, additional payment.

Including the chapels, there were nearly two hundred Christian consecrated buildings in Athens, many of them in ruins or consisting only of bare walls, frequented solely on the anniversaries of the saints to whom they were dedicated; a portrait of the holy owner was placed in them on that occasion, and removed when the solemnity of the day was over. These edifices were, however, largely constructed of ancient fragments and the altar was often a slab of marble with an inscription underneath, supported by a segment of an ancient column or the pedestal of a statue. Elgin found them a fertile source of antiquities, for the Archbishop of Athens granted him permission to inspect all those under his jurisdiction and the mission was able to carry away several curious fragments. The archbishop also presented Elgin's parents-in-law with a marble throne from the old cathedral which, brought back with Elgin's acquisitions and despite shipwreck on the way, is now at Biel in East Lothian. Mrs Nisbet was also rumoured to have picked out a block from the Pnyx (the meeting-place of the Athenian Assembly in antiquity) to be shipped for use as a chimney-piece.

No traveller failed to visit the temple of Theseus (in reality that of Hephaistos), the best-preserved of all the Athenian buildings of the classical age, its sturdy Doric columns apparently fit to endure another two thousand years, the loveliness of its colouring such that the stones looked as if they had been quarried, not from the bed of a rocky mountain, but from the golden light of an Athenian sunset. The sculptured metopes and frieze still remained in position; Fauvel would acidly remark that it was doubtless because they were in too damaged a condition for Elgin's mission to have thought them worth removing. The temple, like so many others, had been converted to Christian use by the Byzantines, considerable destruction having been wrought in the process; as at the Parthenon, several columns had been removed from the east end to allow the building of an apse; the original timber roof tiled with marble had been replaced by an incongruous concrete barrel vault, and the entrance was through a low, iron-plated door on which numerous bullet marks were evidence of wanton Turkish target practice. The little that remained of the marble paving had been removed by a Turk in 1769 to make lime mortar for the house he was building on the road to Eleusis.

The temple was dedicated to St George and had long been a Christian burial-place; it now contained a sad register of those who had succumbed to the health hazards of the Ottoman Empire. There lay the young scholar Tweddell, buried in 1799 by Fauvel, who had had the grave dug in the centre in the illusory hope of finding the remains of Theseus. It remained a sad, sepulchral mound of earth till 1810, when competition between Lusieri, who wished to erect a tombstone with a Latin inscription by Elgin, and Byron and his friends, who procured another marble on which to chisel a Greek epitaph, resulted in the tomb being graced with a double remembrance.

Lady Ruthven's maid Elizabeth Cumming reposed beside him and near by was the grave of Benjamin Gott, an enthusiastic collector; T. M. Phillips was also commemorated, a misguided young man who had quitted Athens in August 1819, a time when disease often raged with violence in the countryside; his name was found scratched on a column of a temple in Arcadia near which he had succumbed. George Watson's Latin epitaph had been composed by Byron, and the much-worn slab can still be seen in the temple floor.

Such a catalogue of deaths was enough to chasten any traveller. None was stricken by the plague, but almost all fell victim to malaria. The mosquito was not then recognised as the carrier, but the curative properties of the red Peruvian bark—quinine—were known and no seasoned visitor journeyed without it. Any other treatment was almost as perilous as the disease. Fauvel maintained that Tweddell had succumbed as a result of curbing his fever in his own way, with vomitives and the powders of Dr James. So when Chateaubriand developed a fever in the wilds near Sunion, spending seventeen hours in delirium, Fauvel sent him a supply of bark and malaga wine; he took a treble dose of both.

The so-called doctors who were constantly about the Morea were highly dangerous; they usually came from the Ionian Islands and had little or no medical training, witness one who had been a druggist's boy, was illiterate, but had some empirical knowledge and was highly extolled for the cures he had performed. The remedies prescribed by superstition were less harmful, as when a Turk dealt with a headache by taking hold of an Englishman's temple with his right hand while an elderly Muslim who sat near by bent down his little finger, reciting a charm. The sufferer felt himself obliged to sacrifice his Christian faith for a moment in favour of politeness and announce that he felt much better, for the Turk was prepared to bend down the other fingers in succession as far as the thumb which, he asserted, was an infallible cure.

No traveller who had had the Greek classics hammered into him at school would fail to visit the Areopagus, the hill on which had once assembled that most ancient and celebrated court of Athens and where Aeschylus had placed the trial of Orestes. Fauvel had discovered there a number of votive tablets sculptured with various parts of the human form, some inscribed with names, all dedicated to Zeus All High. He had been extremely puzzled by such incongruous relics; in the absence of excavating procedures that would have enabled him to distinguish the different layers of occupation of the site, he could not realise that they had not been deposited till Roman times, when Zeus was worshipped there as a healing god.

The Pnyx affords an example of the casual digging-out methods practised by visitors. According to his diary, the nineteen-year-old Earl of Aberdeen walked with Lusieri in the evening of 31 August 1803 and settled to restore the Pnyx; the next day, he walked about to procure antiquities, in particular a damaged inscription from the *disdar*, and then superintended the digging at the Pnyx, copied some inscriptions, and in the evening visited

Fauvel; on 3 September he visited Marathon; on the 5th, he finished his excavations, considering that the Pnyx was now perfectly restored; he also opened a tomb. All that he cleared was a stepped platform, the *bema*; all that he found were some votive tablets similar to Fauvel's.

The Hon Frederick North, later Lord Guilford, chose for his diggings in 1813 the ruins of the library built by Hadrian. A 30ft-deep accumulation of soil and rubbish had to be removed before his workmen reached traces of the 100 Phrygian marble columns that were known to have ringed the court, though none of the decorative statues was found. It is surprising that the Governor of Athens should have granted permission to dig in this area, for his own house and garden occupied a large part of it. North, however, was regarded by the Athenians with feelings rarely given to the passing travellers; his merits as a scholar and his intimate knowledge of modern Greek literature had perhaps done less to connect him with Greece than his intercourse with the people of the country and the reputation for generous and enlightened liberality he had everywhere left behind him. (He is said to have spent £2,000–£3,000 during his stay in Athens.) Later, with continuing liberality, he devoted himself to the creation of a university on Corfu, becoming its first chancellor in 1824. His antiquities have mostly been lost, in particular a famous marble well-head he despatched to his house in London; it was sold as part of the fixtures after his death in 1827, but when the house was later pulled down, it disappeared; it may still be in the foundations of 24 St James's Place.

The Tower of the Winds, the ancient Athenians' weather-vane, sundial and water-clock, was certain to figure in any tour. It was almost hidden from view by the Turkish houses built up against it, and the rubbish of centuries concealed its lower courses. Like other monuments that had been adapted for use as Islamic or Christian holy places, it was comparatively well preserved, having lost only its weather-vane; it had been appropriated by an order of dancing dervishes who performed in it under a chandelier every Friday.

Though space does not permit mention of the influence on western architecture of the discoveries made in Greece, one instance may be mentioned. From Fauvel's casts and drawings of that famous and elegant little edifice, the Monument of Lysicrates, the brothers Trabucci of Paris fabricated an imitation in terracotta that was shown at the Exhibition of Industrial Arts in 1800. Napoleon acquired it and his favourite architect Fontaine set it up in the Park of Saint-Cloud. It was known to the Parisians as the Lantern of Diogenes and a lamp was lit within it at night to let them know when their Consul was in residence. Sadly, it was destroyed in the Franco-Prussian War of 1870.

The antiquarian was well advised not to ignore the modern walls of the town. These had been erected in 1780 as a defence against the pirates and hordes of Albanians who sometimes entered at night threatening pillage; built in seventy-five days at the behest of the Turkish Governor, every material readily to hand had been utilised; in consequence there were exhibited in some places large and obviously ancient blocks of stone and marble, as well as inscriptions, often upside down.

A cornfield surrounded the remains of the temple of Olympian Zeus. The largest in Greece, all but 17 of its 104 gigantic Corinthian columns had disappeared over the centuries. The noble brotherhood remaining were much admired by travellers, who remarked that the hot sun of noon seemed to give them a yellowish tint, while the glow of sunset made them shine like burnished gold; in the sombre shade of the evening they assumed a reddish cast, and when the full moon shone upon their shafts and the night wind sighed through the foliage of their intricate capitals, the long and polished cornice would glitter like silver as the tall pillars flung their black shadows far away. A brick building rested on the architrave of the thirteen columns to the south-east; it had formerly been the aerial residence of a stylite hermit and has now, of course, been removed. Today's prostrate column was overturned by a gale in 1852, but another was wantonly destroyed in 1759 by a Turkish governor; it was undermined and a charge of gunpowder laid, but such was its massive strength that a fourth explosion took place before it fell; it was turned into lime mortar and employed in the construction of the mosque in Monastiraki Square. The temple had also suffered from the Turkish passion for target practice: there was a stone seat near by, about 10ft high, with steps to mount it, on which the Turks were in the habit of sitting to fire at the columns. This, fortunately, did not have the same destructive effect as on the island of Samos, where the few remaining columns of the temple of Hera were being thrown down by the gunnery practice of Turkish men-of-war.

The banks of the Ilyssos provided another sad instance of destruction. Here had stood a small Ionic temple converted into a church, until in 1674 the French ambassador to the Sublime Porte celebrated mass according to the Roman Catholic rite within its precincts; this was regarded as desecration by the Orthodox Greeks, who abandoned it. It became ruinous, but Stuart and Revett were able to draw and measure it for publication in their *Antiquities of Athens*. Its miserably shattered remains were finally removed in 1779; according to a German traveller, the Archbishop of Athens bought it from the Turks and used its materials in the construction of a church in the town.

Yet another loss in this vicinity is recorded. One day, when Dodwell was sketching there, some peasants in ploughing discovered a marble statue; unfortunately not aware of the discovery, Dodwell did not speak to them till he had finished his occupation; he then found that they had already broken the sculpture up and begun to form one of the pieces into a mortar for pounding coffee. Antique marble vases were often put to use in the same way, while the chief peril for large flat stones came from the rough salt that was frequently laid on them to be crushed into particles, a process fatal to marble. Such stones also served the women to beat their clothes upon in washing them, by which means any lettering was almost always obliterated.

It was advisable for visitors to be circumspect in their endeavours to procure sculpture and to conceal their eagerness to possess it. Both Greeks and Turks supposed them to have too much sense to offer large sums for blocks of stone unless these were precious in some way, either as amulets or because they concealed gold or jewels. For instance, a Turk, digging in his garden, discovered a marble statue of Venus, nearly as large as life, and scarcely mutilated. A Frank, to whom it was shown, incautiously offered a large sum for this masterpiece, upon which the Turk refused the bargain and broke the statue in pieces to search for the treasure he imagined it to contain. The parts were put together afterwards and the cast taken from them proved what a loss the fine arts had sustained. It was, however, untrue that the Lion of Chaeronea had suffered a similar fate at the hands of a pasha. It was discovered by Taylor in 1818, broken and half buried, not surprisingly since it had stood 28ft high, traditionally erected by the Thebans to commemorate the Sacred Band of warriors fallen on that battlefield. Taylor engaged some peasants to dig up the head and some limbs and lodged a claim to possession in Athens; when he became civil architect to the Navy, he tried unsuccessfully to have it brought to England in one of HM ships. It was still in much the same state when it came to be restored at the beginning of this century by the Greek Archaeological Society.

The head of a god, a hero or a philosopher ran a considerable risk of being chiselled down into a turban to adorn the tomb of a dead Turk, a practice that inspired an Italian who served as Austrian consul at Salonika; since the Turks used for their tombs the most beautiful pieces of antiquity they could procure, he had no hesitation in appropriating these in his turn. He engaged some bandits who, during the night, stole what he had pointed out to them and transported the fragments to the seashore, leaving them buried in the sand until a ship arrived to transport them to Italy. He continued his operations for some ten years, extending them into the interior and robbing a very considerable number of cemeteries.

The visitor might end his tour of Athens with the valley that had once contained the stadium of Athens and was now a cotton field. It had been completely refurbished in AD 144 by that benefactor of the city, Herodes Atticus, but now there remained only the rubble core, impervious to any tool, that had once supported the tiers of Pentelican marble. Pausanias tells us that Herodes' restoration was more marvellous to see than to hear of; today's is perhaps the reverse.

From there could be viewed, on the slope of the Acropolis, the Choregic Monument of Thrasyllos, a severe Doric portico erected in front of a cave dedicated to Dionysos. The removal by Elgin's mission of the statue that once crowned it is one action that cannot be condemned: it was a hideous Roman addition. The Monument itself was destroyed in a Turkish bombardment during the War of Independence; all that remains is a sad, deserted cave-chapel.

THE 'MUSEUM'

Both Lusieri and Fauvel built themselves houses. Lusieri's was under the north slope of the Acropolis, near the Capuchin monastery; it commanded a delightful prospect and was surrounded by a neat garden. Fauvel's, built in 1813, was much grander, hard by the Doric portico of the Agora, a large French flag flying before it. In its walls were encrusted slabs of marble inscribed with public decrees, funeral farewells, consecrations and records of honourable services rendered in antiquity; the open stairway rested on inscribed marble pages from the register in which Athens had immortalised her history; the mounting-block by the entrance had been the record of some Athenian's bequest of wine for distribution amongst his compatriots during the Panathenaic feast; the garden housed statues and lettered marbles.

The difference between their houses points up a more fundamental dissimilarity: Lusieri never collected or sold antiquities on his own behalf; Fauvel was a dealer with an excellent turnover, and his house—his 'museum'—was, in effect, an emporium for the sale of antiquities. His salary as consul, he would explain, was not sufficient to allow him to satisfy his passion for the arts; he was obliged to get rid of his antiquities, after having enjoyed them, to obtain financial resources to discover others to enjoy anew. That this involved the haphazard dispersal of precious relics sold off as isolated fragments did not concern him or his clients. He shipped antiquities to the busy mart of Smyrna and to France, where Morel d'Arleux, Keeper of Drawings at the Louvre, acted as his agent. He sold to visitors at Athens—one diarist considered it impossible to live there for eight days without being smitten with antiquarianism, the most common symptom of which malady was an insane passion for old halfpence, headless images and handleless jugs which the patient called medals, statues and vases. The English *Milordi* were the best buyers and, during the French wars, almost the only ones; it was not till 1817 that Forbin, Keeper of Antiquities at the Louvre, arrived to buy, for £350, a head, six steles and a bronze urn, now in the museum; but he was soon complaining that English gold left nothing behind for those who could afford only reasonable prices; the prodigalities of a few sons of Albion had awoken the cupidity of the Oriental, and the least antiquity sold for an exorbitant price, not only in Greece, but on the Asian coast and in Egypt.

Pouqueville alleged malpractice: when the rich Greek Corinthian family Notara informed him that they had some bas-reliefs to sell, the Pasha of the Morea pounced and disposed of them himself to an Englishman. Since, said Pouqueville, he himself was not accustomed to snatching the belongings of private persons with the aid of a satrap, he was unable to compete, though he would have refused the offer of the Belvedere Apollo if made under such conditions; but not everyone had such stupid scruples.

Fauvel's antiquities came chiefly from opening tombs, for after 1803 he never stirred far afield. Painted vases, small statues that had once ornamented the shrine of some Athenian home, toys, the amusement of childhood, a mirror that, he said, had perhaps once belonged to Aspasia, a collection of the weights and measures used in ancient Attica, a sling-shot inscribed 'Receive'; everything had been retrieved higgledy-piggledy to be displayed with an equal lack of method. He never tried, for instance, to assign his finds to the different periods of Greek civilisation in an historical perspective: his procedure was, on one occasion, to take any three cinerary urns, sieve the contents and, on finding obols, Charon's fee for ferrying the dead, make a blanket pronouncement that he now had proof that the Greeks placed obols in their tombs; they did, but not until Hellenistic times. His failure to systematise was, of course, far from unique: most collections of his time were just as haphazardly arranged; it has to be remembered that the classification into Stone, Bronze and Iron Ages had not yet even been proposed and that it was generally accepted, on the basis of biblical evidence, that man had been created exactly 4,004 years before the birth of Christ. Archaeology had not been born fully armed like Athene.

To his credit, none the less, are several factual findings. The number and beauty of the painted vases being unearthed in mainland Greece led him to recognise, one of the first to do so, that the so-called Etruscan vases found in such quantity in Italy were in fact of Greek origin, and that the Italians, seeking to enhance their country's artistic renown, had erroneously claimed that all the beautiful artefacts discovered in their country had been created by the native genius. But his discoveries remained isolated facts; like his antiquities, they were little publicised and less correlated.

Though much of his collection was of genuine antique value, many of his cherished possessions had gained a place less for their intrinsic worth than for their rarity or peculiarity, and even natural history had its place. This, again, was not unusual: general collections of his time often contained, besides antiquities, freaks of nature, minerals, weapons and pressed plants; the British Museum was long described as an Exhibition of Antiquities and Natural Curiosities, its entrance flanked by three enormous stuffed giraffes; but such mixtures were becoming outdated.

His collection of coins, one of the most lucrative departments, was in constant turnover—he sold a number of coins to Aberdeen, for instance—even though he was apt to attribute to his specimens a uniqueness they did not always possess.

One of his favourite occupations was constructing models, and for years he worked on one six feet long showing Athens according to the description of ancient writers.

His collection of plaster casts of the sculpture and decorative details of the monuments of Athens was another source of pride, for casts were esteemed not only for the training of artists but for general aesthetic appreciation; the Prince Regent and Pope Pius VII exchanged casts of the Elgin marbles and Niobe and her children, and the rich French sculptor Giraud went specially to Rome to arrange for reproductions so that he could transform his mansion on the Place Vendôme into a museum of casts. Fauvel, indeed, does not seem to have been conscious of the difference between original and reproduction, for he proposed to his government that the extraction of marble from the Pentelic quarries should be organised as in antiquity and blocks shipped to Europe, so that young sculptors could copy his casts as soon as these had been touched up by the best masters. Thus, he thought, the works of art that time was irremediably hastening to fatal decay could be made to live again, young artists could be trained according to the best canons of art, and his government could be enriched.

Fauvel made no lasting contribution to the study of Greek art and architecture during all the long years of his residence at Athens, nor indeed did Lusieri, for neither had received the education nor acquired the knowledge that would have made this possible. Lusieri's knowledge of antiquities was superficial: he considered it unnecessary to send his architectural draughtsmen to the temples of Aegina or Bassae since, he said, both were of the Doric order and it was well known that the true model of this order was met with in the Parthenon; trained architects were soon to discover that both temples possessed unique features of great beauty and interest. Fauvel, as corresponding member of the Institut, faithfully and usefully kept Paris informed of all archaeological discoveries in his area, but he was less reliable where tasks requiring knowledge of the classics was concerned, such as copying Greek inscriptions, and he had to be requested on occasion to re-work his somewhat mediocre reproductions. He himself had no illusions as to his abilities in this field and was invariably ready to hand his transcriptions over with good grace to the savants, though he could not resist expressing malign pleasure at the erudite battles that would doubtless result from their varying interpretations and reconstitutions. He was far from being the only one to copy carelessly: accusations of arbitrary additions and unfounded guesswork frequently flew. His inadequate knowledge of the classics also affected his topography, and he seldom committed himself to indentifying the ruins marked on the maps he prepared, preferring with prudent reserve to leave this to scholars like his friend Barbié du Bocage, the famous geographer, whose maps were published in several travelogues.

It is sad that he should never have succeeded in organising his knowledge into publishable form. The difficulty was that, though he had the necessary facts, he lacked the erudition needed to extend and embellish his text with numerous and learned citations from classical authors; for no travelogue was regarded as acceptable without copious quotation from the ancients and the whiff of midnight oil comes from the pages of many a visitor. He seems to have been content to allow the travellers who passed through Athens to profit from his knowledge and discoveries, even when they published them without acknowledgement.

Fauvel seems rarely to have sold his drawings except, reluctantly, in 1799 when the Franco-Turkish war seemed about to lead to his incarceration. He then ceded a number to the English traveller Hawkins, but many more to the young scholar Tweddell, when some fifty drawings stepped from his portfolio into Tweddell's at a price of £100.

Lusieri could not thus dispose of his productions which, according to his agreement with Elgin, were his patron's property. Furthermore, he seems seldom to have finished them. He generally had several panoramic views in a progressive state from various quarters of the town so that, let the wind blow where it would, he could always secure for himself a comfortable spot; but he attempted an accuracy and minuteness of delineation that was hardly consistent with the mutable nature of such objects and the brevity of human life: before one part of his outline was complete, the growth of trees or alteration of buildings made it necessary to erase another. Fauvel commented that one half of his time was spent in drawing and the other in rubbing out. A certain number seem, none the less, to have been completed, for a visitor saw examples that were exquisitely finished and Félicité Roque was permitted to copy at least one. We shall never know for certain, for his entire Athenian portfolio was lost on its way back to England in the wreck of HMS *Cambrian* in 1828.

Extraordinary as it may seem, he had never sent Elgin a single drawing. His health was partly to blame: after 1812, he suffered from a most painful rheumatism that eased somewhat only around 1818; but his natural tendency towards procrastination and inability to 'finish' were more significant. It is, however, understandable that Elgin should have become impatient, finally seeking to terminate the connection by asking Lusieri to send the drawings, completed or not. Lusieri was deeply hurt and had still not complied at the time of his death in 1821.

He was buried in the garden of the Capuchin monastery and a tablet was placed over his grave bearing an inscription to the effect that it was erected by the English at Athens as a tribute to his talents and in grateful remembrance of his services.

ACCOMMODATION FOR VISITORS

Where did all the visitors stay during their residence at Athens?

Lusieri never received guests, but Fauvel sometimes provided a rather uncomfortable couch for his compatriots. Chateaubriand was given a room full of casts of the Parthenon sculptures and hung with views of the Theseion, drawings of the Propylaea and maps of Attica; there were marbles on one table, coins on another, and little heads and vases in terracotta on a third; someone swept up a bit of ancient dust and a camp bed was put up in the middle. A later denizen found his bed made up against the wall; on the first night, hardly had he laid his head on the pillow than he felt a hand stroking his hair; he seized it, trembling with fright; it was marble, and belonged to a Venus that, hung on a line, dangled against the wall and was still moving from the shaking he had given her when he threw himself on the bed. Anette, an Albanian, was the housekeeper, and when she had set the table under a trellis in the garden, the guests would feast on doves from Sunion and drink wine from the islands.

The English agent, Logotheti, was equally hospitable, even moving out of his house to accommodate the Elgins. Her ladyship's pianoforte was set in the main room and the long first-floor gallery was turned into a living-room where the party breakfasted and sat reading, writing and arranging coins.

Some of the Athenians let rooms in their houses. Such apartments were usually about 22ft long and 12ft wide; a divan covered with a multitude of cushions surrounded one end and served as a bed; glazed wooden casements were put up during the winter, for keeping warm was a problem when snow covered even Mount Hymettos, and the charcoal braziers, whose fumes, it was hoped, would disperse through the cracks in the floorboards, were small comfort.

Theodorulla Mina Makri's house was much patronised, for, the relict of a Scots doctor, she was accustomed to Frank travellers. Her daughter-in-law Theodora Makri's rooms on Odhos Theklas were also well known: she was the widow of the former British agent and mother of three charming daughters much admired by visitors who lodged at the 'Consulina's', including Byron; his friend Hobhouse stayed at Dr Vitali's next door, a passage being opened in the wall between the two dwellings. Madame Masson's house was popular, as was that of Demetrios Zographos, and the Capuchin monks were always hospitable to travellers at the monastery by the Monument of Lysicrates: Leake stayed there, as did Byron on his second visit.

Some travellers preferred to rent a house and cater for themselves. Lady Hester Stanhope did so, and quickly transformed it into a comfortable home where a small, select company met every evening. Odhos Ermou came to be regarded as the Chaussée d'Antin of Athens: Caroline, Princess of Wales, took rooms just off it in 1816; General Church, of War of Independence fame, Finlay the historian, and the English and Russian ministers later took up residence there. Farther north, good houses were to be found in Odhos Tholou, in particular the eighteenth-century dwelling that was bought and repaired by the architect Schaubert in 1829, then rented out by him to house Athens's first university in 1837; it is now a taverna.

THE ENVIRONS OF ATHENS

The collector who intended to search for antiquities outside Athens needed first to hire a horse for his excursions; travelling on foot was regarded by the inhabitants as degrading, and neither Turk nor Greek, above a certain rank, would submit to be seen as pedestrians otherwise than in pacing through the streets of their towns. A Turk meeting an Englishman on foot a few miles from Athens inquired if the traveller was a gentleman Frank, which he said he much doubted, as no gentleman would walk if he had paras enough to pay for a horse.

Though shabby-looking animals, these horses were generally tolerable hacks; one traveller, however, complained that his mount would not go on unless given a loose rein and could not stand on its legs unless the bridle was held tight; in other respects, as the owner remarked, it was unexceptionable. A good saddle was an essential item of equipment, for the wooden pack-saddles, formed of bars inserted in triangular frames and girded by worsted bands to the horse, were not only a form of torture but tore the Franks' inexpressibles on the multitudinous nails that protruded everywhere from their flanks. Even Turkish riding saddles were uncomfortable, for the short leathers bent the rider's legs under his chin, the raised front rammed him in the chest and the high back dug him in the kidneys. Byron and Hobhouse, who must be classed among the more luxurious travellers, took with them four English saddles and bridles.

The baggage was carried in sacks, saddle bags or string baskets slung on either side of the pack-animals: quilts of woven cotton and camp beds, cooking utensils and provisions, the *Milordi*'s portmanteaux, carpet bags and hat boxes were stuffed in or piled on top. All this 'English comfort' was eschewed by some travellers, understandably when one reads that Byron and Hobhouse were never less than two hours getting fairly on their way: there would be a long quarrel between the different owners of the horses, each being anxious that his own beast should not be overloaded; then there would be a want of ropes; then a high dirty pad had to be inserted between the unfamiliar English saddle and the horse's spine. At the opposite extreme was Chateaubriand, who in his *course effrénée* through Greece appears to have set out most mornings before dawn and whose equipment consisted of a carpet to sit on, several shawls to wrap his head in at night, and a coffee pot.

Opening tombs soon became a favourite pursuit of the collector, for it had all the attractions of hunting or of a lottery. The graves near the Piraeus, though completely concealed by weeds and bushes, were so numerous that discovery was easy; they were cut in the rocks, their depth being usually four or five feet, and when, after several vain essays, the sound of pickaxes announced a cavity, joy reigned. The opening operation was performed by breaking the *trapeza*, or cover, with a large hammer, and then overturning it with a strong pole as a lever; ten workmen could open thirty tombs in the course of nine hours. The contents were then shovelled out, the best objects being retained and the rest thrown away. Opening a tumulus spared some of this trouble: the workmen would simply dig down from the top, collecting *en route* a fragmented hotch-potch of decorated vases, terracotta figures, calcinated bones, bronze and gold-leaf decorative sheathing, mirrors and swords.

The most famous tomb of the Piraeus was that attributed by tradition and Fauvel to Themistocles, situated at the extremity of the Akte peninsula. All that could be seen was a double stone coffin cut out of the rock, whose broken sides gave fine ingress and egress to every wave that the Aegean might roll over it; near by lay an overturned column that had once marked the entrance to the harbour. Elgin's mission had as little justification in attributing to Aspasia a tomb they excavated near by. Such casual attributions were common and it was some years before their perpetrators came to be condemned for deluding themselves and the world; when nothing was known about a thing, announced one critic, it was better to say so.

Sandford Graham, with whom Byron exchanged an excellent Greek lexicon for a small gem, was an ardent collector of decorated vases and is said to have acquired about a thousand from Athenian sites in 1810. One of the best-known retrievals was that of the Levant merchant Burgon who, in 1813, unearthed an archaic cemetery containing some fifty burials from which he retained at least the black figure amphora that bears his name in the British Museum.

The Phaelleen Fields, the vast necropolis that stretched between the foot of Mount Hymettus and the sea, was a fertile source of antiquities and a particularly happy hunting-ground for Fauvel. In association with the merchant Gropius, he discovered and sold an inscription to a Dutchman, Colonel Rottiers, that is now in the Leyden museum; the broken pieces of three particularly interesting vases went to the Prussian ambassador who presented them to his king; a sculptured lion, bought by the French Admiral Halgan, enriched the Louvre. Gropius, having found some coffins in exceptionally dry earth, had rules and set-squares for artists made from them in the hope that the thousand-year-old wood would not warp.

The most famous burial site of all was the tumulus at Marathon. This unmistakable mound had been discovered by Fauvel almost by accident when, having unearthed three good Roman busts* near the ruins of a monumental gateway, he had been searching the vicinity for further remains. He drove a trench half-way into the west side of the 30ft-high barrow but found nothing; it seemed therefore likely that it had contained only the ashes of the 192 Athenian fallen who had been accorded the unusual honour of burial on the site of their victory over the invading Persians. The funerary slabs bearing the names of the dead had long since disappeared; only flowers now adorned the

*Two are now in the Louvre; that of L. Verus is in the British Museum.

mound: anemones, crocus and jonquils guarded its base while its slopes were covered with asphodel whose tall pink spikes stood erect in defiance of the breeze and among whose petals the bees murmured securely.

Disused wells were a notorious repository of antiquities. In the substratum of one, Clarke found no less than thirty-seven entire pottery vessels; he selected the best specimens and threw away the rest. Hobhouse retrieved two rather mediocre Aphrodites from another, while a third visitor's activities had a useful by-product; he restored to the Athenians, to their great joy, a very fine spring of water, which burst forth upon the removal of the rubbish by which the well had been filled.

The churches and chapels that dotted the Attic plain were also put to contribution: one collector came across the sculptured torso of a young man almost buried under some rubbish in a deserted edifice; he could not bear, he said, to leave it there to its fate; he removed it, leaving a small donation.

At an easy ride from Athens lay Daphni, the site of an ancient sanctuary of Apollo, now appropriated by a monastery that huddled inside battlemented defences. The Turks frequently used the church as a baiting-place, as they did any building with a doorway large enough to admit a horse, and they had disfigured the huge Byzantine mosaic of Our Saviour in the vault of the dome; the eyes had been perforated by the bullets of Islamic fanaticism in hatred of the watching gaze of such representations. The Greeks had not been guiltless of vandalism: pirates had attacked the monastery and, imagining the gold ground of the mosaic to be precious metal, had removed the tesserae. A few architectural members of the ancient temple had been re-utilised in the walls of the church, and Elgin's agents prised out and appropriated two Ionic capitals, a column base and part of a shaft. (Some pillars and carved fragments still remain today.) The edifice was not considered at that time to contain anything else worthy of observation, for disapprobation of Byzantine church architecture and decoration was general; it was considered to be a barbarous style that had pervaded Greece since the times of

Justinian, characterised by domes and ugly arches that disgusted the eye accustomed to the simple, noble and majestic buildings of the ancients. Equally condemned were the paintings and mosaics, dismissed as caricatures of praying saints, delineated with complete disregard for the rules of perspective on staring blue, yellow or red backgrounds. Neglect, if not destruction, of such remains was evident everywhere. The Greeks were forced to purchase permission from the Turks to repair their churches, and often hesitated to do so from fear that this might provide an excuse for further exactions; sadly, it seemed that much of the material evidence of a Christian faith that had survived centuries of Turkish occupation, and done so much to hold the people together, was doomed to disappear.

The few ruined temples that remained above ground within easy reach of Athens did not escape the collectors. Eleusis, as we shall see in the next chapter, lost its statue; Rhamnous, on the east coast, once famous for the worship of Nemesis, was creamed by Gandy, a member of the 1811 expedition sent out by the Society of Dilettanti; he discovered and appropriated there a fragment of a colossal head, probably from the statue of the god, as well as a female torso and a votive relief. The temple at Cape Sounion had only decorative mouldings to lose, and lost them. The off-shore island of Kea yielded, from the remains of its temple of Apollo, the larger half of a colossal statue of the deity and various other fragments, but at least there could be no question of removing the colossal lion carved in the living rock near the chief town; it was, and is, 20ft long and 9ft high.

4

ELEUSIS

Edward Daniel Clarke had the great good fortune to be appointed, when only thirty, as travelling tutor to John Cripps, an amiable young man of independent means who had just graduated from Jesus College, Cambridge, where Clarke held the bursarship. France and Italy being closed by the French wars, tutor and pupil set off in 1799 for northern Europe, then made their way via Constantinople to Greece, the first Grand Tourists to venture into a country that had in a manner been forgotten by the rest of Europe. Though at first sorely disappointed by the rack and ruin that confronted them, they were soon in raptures over the wonderful scenery and the antiquities lying about almost for the taking at Athens. Having secured some marbles of doubtful authenticity, they set out to tour the Morea—the Peloponnese.

Here they confined their acquisitions to more portable objects such as coins. Few travellers could resist buying these, little as they often knew of the speciality. One Englishman frankly considered his collection to be as pretty a set of trash as a gentleman need have; some of his specimens would, he thought, admit of a learned dispute as to whether they were intended to represent Jupiter the Thunderer or the Venus of Paphos. Forgeries were not uncommon, and foundries are said to have been established later for the purpose at Athens and Argos, the owners even having the impudence to offer their wares burning hot from the furnace.

73

They can perhaps hardly be blamed, in view of the method of acquisition employed by Clarke and Cripps. These gentlemen discovered that the peasants would not readily part with the silver coins that decorated the head-dresses of the women, who attached them to a small cap on their foreheads and entwined them in their hair; however, newly coined paras, though of base metal and worth only a fraction of the silver ones, could be used to tempt them to sell. Clarke and Cripps provided themselves with a small cargo of these coins fresh from the mint and in exchange for this shoddy but shining bait obtained many very curious coins in silver, at least one being of uncommon rarity; if they had attempted to pay in old and dulled coin, they said, they would have obtained nothing under a large number of piastres.

Three other English travellers made a less blatantly profiteering bargain at Delphi. A sort of town crier was in the habit of mounting the roof of a house and informing the village and the echoes of Parnassos of whatever was going on in trade; on his offering his services to the *Milordi*, they requested him to tell the inhabitants to bring anything they had to sell; one of them was thus enabled to buy for £2 a gold coin that later proved to be very valuable. They next offered a reward for one of the vultures of the Parnassos; the commission was duly executed and they found the bird's wings to measure nine feet from tip to tip, thus explaining the roar like a hurricane caused when one of them passed overhead.

One of the best collections of coins was that owned by Colonel Rooke. He was a very singular man, of large property, who had retired about 1800, acquiring a residence in most of the islands of the archipelago—in some, a room at a friend's house, and in others a house of his own—but he lived generally in his boat, of which he had furnished the interior with every luxury, including a good library. He made it a fixed rule to sail before the wind for, as he was equally at home in all the islands, it was a matter of perfect indifference to him to which of them he steered his course. He died in Cyprus about 1813, leaving to two maiden sisters in England all his property and his curiosities, but the latter were apparently lost. It is possible that he was the same as the gentleman who often made Scio his favourite abode on account of the fineness of the air and was said to indulge himself with an air bath by regularly walking some hours in a state of nudity on the top of a high mountain.

The most expert and successful collector, however, was Fauvel's friend Cousinéry, who spent many years as a consular official in the Levant, mostly at Salonika. He acquired in all some 26,000 coins; in 1811, he sold a collection to Prince Ludwig of Bavaria for £6,900, and later another for £3,500; in 1817, he disposed of yet another to Austria for £1,700, while a fourth went to France in 1821. He had one great antiquarian virtue: unlike amateur plunderers, he recorded the provenance of his coins.

When Clarke and Cripps stopped at Eleusis on their way back from the Morea, they found a specimen of unique beauty open to capture if only they could move it.

Eleusis was one of the most famous sanctuaries of antiquity. It was there that Demeter had paused in her search for Persephone, borne away to the underworld by Pluto; it was there that she had disclosed her divinity and commanded the people to build her a temple in which she had shut herself up, refusing to see the other gods and causing a most dreadful and cruel year for mankind over all the earth by refusing to allow the seed to sprout. Faced with the destruction of the human race through bitter famine, Zeus had recalled Persephone from the lower world for part of each year. She had been brought back by Hermes, who had halted his fiery horses at Eleusis, where mother and daughter had been reunited with great rejoicing. Before returning to Olympus, Demeter had made fruit spring from the rich land so that the whole earth was filled with leaves and flowers. She had then revealed to the King of Eleusis the conduct of her rites and the content of her Mysteries.

Over the centuries, Demeter's temple had been many times rebuilt, each time more splendidly, and shrines, courts and gated walls had been added to form a splendid sanctuary for the performance of the Mysteries. Their secrets have never been unveiled, for despite the thousands of Greek and, later, Roman citizens who were initiated into them—they continued to be celebrated well into the Christian era—not one divulged their content.

By 1800, all that remained of the sanctuary was a confused spread of broken columns, fallen architraves and toppled walls, where wild flowers hung in festoons across each crumbling stone. Dotted about were some thirty mud-brick, flat-roofed cottages, dominated by a tower where resided the Turkish overlord. The remains of the outer gate of the precinct, constructed on the model of the Propylaea at Athens, were still identifiable, as were those of the inner gateway, or Lesser Propylaea, that had consisted of two parallel walls enclosing a paved passageway, entered through a porch supported by Corinthian columns. It had been built for a Roman consul, Appius Claudius Pulcher, as a dedicatory embellishment of the sanctuary about 50 BC, but not completed till after his death by his nephews. At the exit, giving on to the sanctuary proper, stood the upper part of a statue thought to be of Demeter herself, in colossal majesty among the mouldering vestiges of her once splendid sanctuary. She was, sadly, in a very ruined state, her face and part of her neck having fallen off. But the sculpture on the cylindrical basket she carried on her head was still fine; the heads of wheat, the poppies, and the kernos or sacred vessel used in the Eleusinian cult were easily recognisable, and the drapery of her chiton, secured between the breasts with a Gorgon's-head clasp, had obviously been finished with the greatest elegance and labour.

She had been identified by several earlier visitors, who had all praised her damaged beauty. A Venetian admiral was said to have attempted to abduct her, but had been repulsed by main force when the local inhabitants armed themselves to defend their divinity. For they regarded her with a very high degree of superstitious veneration, attributing to her presence the fertility of their land; they heaped around her the manure intended for their fields so that at times she stood in a dunghill up to her ears. What would become of their corn, they asked, if the old lady with the basket on her head was removed? The very mention of such a thing was regarded as equal to bringing the moon from its orbit.

Such superstitions, so prevalent amongst both Greeks and Turks, were linked to the universal belief in the evil eye; it was thought that this spirit or invisible power was grieved at all prosperity, groaned at success, was indignant at a plentiful harvest or at the fecundity of flocks, murmured even against heaven for having made a young girl handsome. In consequence, no one thought of congratulating another on having beautiful children, and admiration of a neighbour's horse was avoided, for the evil eye might instantly afflict the children with leprosy or the horse with lameness. If, however, in complimenting beauty, care was taken to talk of garlic or to spit, the evil charm was broken. Garlic was in fact the great specific: it was hung up in any house newly built and decorated every ship as a preservative against tempest.

Men could themselves draw down curses on an enemy by means of the anathema. An injured party would take a quantity of stones and place them in a heap in a conspicuous part of a road, cursing his foe as he laid each one; as no man was supposed to be so anathematised without good reason, it became the duty of all good citizens to add at least one stone and its consequent curse to the heap, so that it often increased to a considerable size. A different system was employed when, if a girl had two suitors, the unsuccessful lover had recourse to charms as a last resource. He tied the locks of his hair, reciting: 'I tie A and B, and the Devil in the middle'; and by every knot deferred the bridegroom's happiness for a night. This tremendous operation being made known to the unhappy husband, he, through credulity and shame, became not infrequently the accomplice in effecting his own misfortune. One man who suffered this calamity for the first month of his marriage was released only by the repeated prayers and holy water of his chaplain.

Many of the superstitions were feminine. Near the Pnyx at

Athens was a slope that had been worn even and slippery by the effects of a singular persuasion prevalent amongst the females of both Christian and Muslim religions: they believed that by sliding uncovered down this stone they increased their chances of bringing forth male children and of obtaining an easy delivery; Franks who saw them at this exercise viewed it as not only disagreeable but indeed rather perilous. Another superstition-haunted place was Athens's stadium: when the young women wanted a happy marriage, the return of a husband or the health of a child, they tied a piece of money into an embroidered handkerchief with a length of red cotton and put it on the ancient circuit with a little honey, a saucer of milk, bread and almonds; as they left, they invoked the Fates, chanting: 'You who preside over the destiny of the universe, take care also of my destiny.'

It is not surprising that people on whom superstition had such a hold should have attributed unearthly power to the ancient remains with which they were surrounded. However much the *Milordi* might scoff, they found they had to take account of such beliefs if antiquities were to be acquired.

MOVING A MASS OF MARBLE

Clarke and Cripps determined to acquire the statue of Demeter and ship her to England, a daunting project, for she weighed over two tons.

They opened their campaign by approaching the priest of the village not only in order to purchase the statue but to induce him to influence the people to allow her to be removed. He informed them, however, that it would first be necessary to obtain a firman from the Turkish Governor of Athens. Luckily, their janissary, Ibrahim, was a kinsman of the Governor and promised all the assistance in his power. Next morning, he waited on his relative and communicated the Englishmen's designs. The Governor acceded to the request but upon the express condition that he be given a small English telescope belonging to Lusieri. Though Clarke was, of course, a friend of the artist, this opposed a very serious obstacle to his plans because it meant divulging the secret of his undertaking to the person who was at the moment employed in collecting everything of the kind for Elgin. There was no time to lose, however, for the Governor might soon mention the matter to the English consul, Logotheti, who, not unnaturally putting the interests of ambassador Elgin first, would, Clarke believed, instantly try to frustrate the project. Finally, it was decided to make Lusieri acquainted with the whole affair, and that gentleman not only resigned his telescope upon the promise of receiving another from England, but undertook to present it himself to the Governor and persuade the latter to observe silence with the consul. The firman was thus obtained, and very cheaply too: some years before, an Englishman had had to part with a handsome snuff-box containing several gold coins merely to get permission to dig and measure at Eleusis. It is, of course, possible that Lusieri complied so readily because he expected Clarke to fail in removing the statue.

Now a new difficulty arose. The ferry-boat that plied between the island of Salamis and the mainland appeared to be the only means of conveying the enormous marble to the Piraeus from the Eleusinian shore, for it was exceptionally large and well-made. But the English consul controlled the ferry-boat because he rented the island for £150 a year from the Turks; it was therefore necessary to apply to him. Such a request, as might be expected, excited Logotheti's curiosity to the highest degree; but after many questions as to the object for which the boat was required, Clarke was able to lull his suspicions; or, if he had any notion of the tutor's intentions, he probably believed, like Lusieri, that all attempts to remove the Demeter would be made in vain.

So Clarke returned successful to Eleusis, only to encounter a situation that nearly put an end to the undertaking. While the villagers were discussing the means of removal with the janissary Ibrahim, an ox loosed from the yoke came and placed itself before the statue and, after butting with its horns for some time against the marble, ran off with considerable speed, bellowing, into the plain. Instantly a general murmur prevailed, and several women joining in the clamour, it was with difficulty that any proposal could be made. They had always been famous for their corn, the villagers cried, and the fertility of the land would cease when the statue was gone. It was late at night before these scruples were removed.

The following morning, the people assembled and stood round the statue, but no one ventured to begin to dig it out of the ground; they believed that the arm of any person would fall off who should dare to touch it or to disturb its position. Presently, however, the priest of Eleusis, partly induced by entreaty and partly terrified by the menaces of Ibrahim, put on his canonical vestments as for a ceremony of high mass and, descending into the hollow where the statue remained upright after the rubbish round it had been taken away, gave the first blow with a pickaxe for the removal of the soil, so that the people might be convinced that no calamity would befall the labourers. The work then went on briskly enough.

The next problem was to transport the statue from the village down to the coast, a declivity of about half a mile. Clarke and Cripps had been able to buy in Athens only a rope of twisted herbs and some large nails; fortunately, they found at Eleusis several long poles, an axe, and a small saw about six inches in length; with these, the stoutest of the poles were cut and the pieces nailed in a triangular form. The villagers dug the earth from round the statue and the immense mass of marble began to incline from its perpendicular; the triangular frame was placed so that, as the statue was lowered by the rope round it, it came gradually to rest upon the frame. With the remainder of the poles, rollers were made over which the frame might move; ropes were then fastened to each extremity of the foremost beam. A hundred peasants had been collected from the village and neighbourhood of Eleusis, and nearly fifty boys; some of them were ranged on each side to pull on the ropes; others were employed, with levers, to raise the frame when rocks or large stones opposed its progress; the boys were engaged in taking up the rollers as fast as the machine left them and in placing them again in the front. In this manner, at midday, the statue reached the brow of the hill above the old port; the descent towards the shore, although among ruins and obstructed by large stones, was more easy. Thus a mass of marble weighing two tons was moved to the sea in about nine hours, achieving a pace almost as fast as a snail.

New difficulties now arose. The ferry-boat had arrived from Salamis, attended by four monks, but they seemed perfectly panic-stricken when they were told that it was the intention to ship the statue in their vessel. First, it was found that the water near to the shore was too shallow to admit the approach of the boat; then it was realised that the old quay of Eleusis could not be used, for, consisting of immense stone blocks stretching out into deeper water, it was in such a ruined state that several wide chasms appeared in it through which the water flowed; across these chasms it would be necessary to construct temporary bridges, but there was no timber for the purpose.

At this critical moment, when Clarke was preparing to abandon the undertaking, a large vessel made her appearance, sailing between Salamis and the Eleusinian coast. He instantly pushed off in a boat and hailed her; and, the captain consenting to come ashore, he not only hired the ship to take the statue to Smyrna but also engaged the assistance of the crew, with their boats and rigging, to help in its removal. They worked with spirit and skill and made the rest of the operation a mere amusement. At sunset, the statue was stationed at the utmost extremity of the pier-head.

Early the following day, two boats belonging to the vessel and the Salamis ferry were placed alongside each other, between the vessel and the pier: planks were laid across, so as to form a kind of stage upon which the sailors might work with blocks and ropes. A small cable was warped round the statue, and, twelve blocks being brought to act all at once, the goddess was raised almost to the yard-arm whence, after remaining suspended a short time, she was lowered into the hold. The Eleusinians taking leave of her, the vessel sailed for Smyrna, where the marble was trans-shipped to the merchantman *Princessa*.

Not surprisingly, the superstitious villagers of Eleusis predicted that the ship bearing their Demeter to the West would be wrecked. Their augury was duly fulfilled in the loss of the *Princessa*, though she conveniently ran aground on the Sussex coast near Beachy Head, not far from Cripps's estate, the manor of Stantons, where his father was at the time residing. This gentleman hastened immediately to the spot and, by his timely interference and care, saved the Demeter and her companion marbles as well as the assorted booty that had been garnered by the travellers. Clarke's filled seventy-six cases containing more than 1,000 Greek coins, some 6,000 foreign plants, and a large collection of minerals, insects, drawings, maps and charts; Cripps had even more.

The marbles were Clarke's great pride, but his swans turned out to be mostly geese. A fragment he obtained on the Acropolis, far from being part of a Parthenon metope, was really a piece of unremarkable and rather ugly gravestone; an inscribed marble that he purchased in Athens 'from under the very nose of Elgin's chaplain and his host of Gothic plunderers' was not the tomb of the famous Euclid as he assumed; his statue of Pan turned out to be only a decorative column from a balustrade.

Finally, Demeter's statue. It was securely placed upon a pedestal, with all due form and honours, in the most conspicuous part of the vestibule of the public library at Cambridge on 1 July 1803; the names of Clarke and Cripps were, by the desire of the university, inscribed upon the base. But it was soon suspected that the statue was only a colossal caryatid, dating from the Roman period. Clarke protested vigorously against such base suspicions and had a theoretical restoration of his beloved statue drawn by the well-known sculptor Flaxman, representing her as a seated goddess. This he published, accompanied by all the erudite evidence he could muster, but to no purpose. She was indeed only a caryatid, whose better-preserved sister is now in the museum at Eleusis.

Unlike other collectors whom we shall meet later, Clarke and Cripps made no profit from their marbles; all were donated to their university, Cripps having so generously borne most of the freight charges—the marbles themselves had cost practically nothing. This meant that the Demeter, however false, was immediately available for the edification of the general public instead of disappearing into oblivion like her daughter Persephone, to some inaccessible English nobleman's seat. (Complaints were rife that the dispersal of the best antiquities around the English countryside was such that it was difficult to view more than a fraction of what existed, added to which, the servants of the great houses were apt to expect gratuities beyond the reach of the humble purse of the visiting student.) The donation of the Demeter marks, in fact, the new trend towards public display of such antiquities: from then on, all the major acquisitions from Greece came to rest in the museums of London, Paris and Munich. The day of the great private collector of marbles was almost over.

After the removal of the Demeter, the ruins of Eleusis remained almost undisturbed for some years, despite Elgin's suggestion that the site could be dealt with in a day, could be measured and dug, with the antiquities it was desired to remove sawn into transportable shape. Such failure to appreciate the time required for the most superficial examination of a site was not then unusual, though somewhat extreme in this case. It is hardly necessary to add that Lusieri did nothing.

A few years later, Dodwell found the inhabitants of Eleusis still lamenting the loss of their statue; they assured him that since her departure their abundance of crops had disappeared. However, when the sceptical Hobhouse visited the site in 1810, he found that the plain had lost nothing of its former fertility; the inhabitants pointed out the trench whence the statue had been dug without evincing any signs of regret for their loss.

The 1811 Expedition of the Society of Dilettanti, Gell and his friend Craven, with the artists Bedford and Gandy, projected a serious study of the site, but while a village covered it they could do little more than confirm that Demeter's great temple, the Telesterion, had been built to a different plan from that of the characteristic Greek temple. The latter had been regarded as the house of the cult statue, which stood in a hall or cella surrounded externally by colonnades; sacrifices were made at altars in the forecourt and the worshippers did not normally enter the cella. The Telesterion, however, since the Mysteries had been enacted in front of crowds of initiates, had consisted of a huge enclosed building without colonnades, though a stoa had been built in front of it by Philo, a few courses of whose supporting wall were still visible above the rubbish of centuries. Gell's party attempted to dig down to the Telesterion foundations, uncovering in the process the marble pavement to the front; finding it very thin and much broken, they removed it to disclose the earlier pavement beneath and, with the casual abandon of their time, allowed the peasants to carry away the fragments of the upper pavement for use as roof tiles. One of their English servants, who passed his time in digging for the artists, was overjoyed at having part of a 'peppermint' (pediment).

It is from Craven that we have a description of the conditions under which antiquarians of the time worked when he describes the 'Dilly' Expedition's occupations on a wet February day. He pictures Gell sitting on the floor of their rented cottage making a map of Eleusis and fighting the splashing of the rain that beat in upon his paper through the only window they could suffer to have open; Craven reclined opposite on his folding bed, his table consisting of a pair of blue trousers bundled up so that he might catch the few rays of light that were to be had and, at the same time, the many fleas that appeared inclined to read his letter; at his feet lay Bedford, in one of those painful attitudes that make one feel the cruel inconvenience of one's own legs, mending the fractures of broken columns and architraves by drawing them in the perfect state in which they would be published by the 'Dilly'; Gandy was trying in vain to make a writing desk lie flat and steady on top of a small round trunk; the perspective was filled by avenues of pots and pans, garlands of onions, and draperies of dusty cobwebs.

They were lucky to have had a room to themselves. Such cot-

Page 85 *(left)* Tower of the Winds, Athens; *(right)* Eleusis Demeter, drawn restored by Flaxman

Page 86 (*above*) Bay of Eleusis; (*below*) Temple at Sunion

tages, constructed of mud walls with a coating of plaster and a thatched roof, usually consisted only of a single room divided by a low partition; in one half slept the oxen and asses used on the farm; in the other, the hosts and their guests, one door serving both apartments, the rafters adorned with restless cocks and hens, incessantly cackling and crowing. Furniture was regarded as unnecessary except for an occasional chest; bedsteads were as rare as carriage roads, and bare floor-boards or the naked earth were the usual resting-place of the traveller, whose camp-bed or thick cotton quilts soon proved their utility. Chimneys were virtually unknown; instead there was a hole in the roof. In winter, the fire was kindled in the middle of the floor and some of the smoke went out of the hole. None the less, most travellers preferred such quarters to the khans or inns that were to be found on the main routes, for these were usually horribly nasty.

There were exceptions, of course: the houses of the consuls at such ports as Patras; at Corinth with the hospitable Greek family Notara; and at Levadhia on the road to Delphi, where the house of another rich Greek, Logotheti, was always open to them. Really luxurious accommodation was to be found with the Turkish pashas, Ali of Jannina in particular; one visitor remarked that he would probably never again lie on so splendid a bed as that which had just been brought from the pasha's harem by two of the black eunuchs: the cover of the mattress and the counterpane were embroidered with gold, the sheets were of worked silk and the pillow of the same, with a splendid border.

But no matter where the traveller slept, execrable insects, the curse of every night in all the Orient, abounded: in the houses and inns, bugs rained from the ceiling and fleas jumped from the cracks in the badly jointed floors; in the cottages, they crept out of the walls and leapt from the earthen floor; they attacked in the fields and scrublands and in hidden caves that one would have expected to be the retreat only of nymphs; the surroundings of venerable ruins were their sites of predilection, because the shepherds and their flocks were in the habit of resting there, and the traveller could find his legs blackened with fleas in the

Treasury of Atreus and the gallery of Tiryns. It has to be remembered, however, that bugs and fleas were the cause of many broken nights in Western Europe also; the *désagréments* of Eastern travel were not sufficient to act as a deterrent even to the amateur antiquarian.

5

THE MOREA

THE WESTERN TOURIST

Collectors and curious travellers fanned out over Greece, their guides to the topography and classical sites at first only the ancient writers such as Pausanias, Strabo and Herodotus. Modern maps were either non-existent or notoriously unreliable.

Pausanias was the greatest help. It is a peculiar piece of good fortune that, from the wreckage of classical literature, his *Description of Greece* should have come down to us practically entire, for it presents an eye-witness account of the state of Greece in the second century of our era and may have been intended as a guide-book for the travellers of the day.

After 1800 came the topographical travellers, describing each mile of the routes throughout Greece so that future visitors would be able not only to find their way on roads that were often nothing better than tracks frequently interrupted, but at the same time identify the ancient sites and buildings. Pouqueville was the first to publish: his *Voyage en Morée* came out in 1805; Gell's detailed itineraries appeared from 1810 onwards; Hobhouse's account of his travels with Byron was printed in 1813 and Dr Holland's travelogue in 1815; Dodwell did not publish until 1819, while Leake's travels were not out until after 1821. However, by 1830, Conder's *Modern Traveller* could include two useful volumes on Greece.

Tourists were well-advised to obtain a firman—a letter from the Sublime Porte—or a *boujoudery*—a similar document from a local pasha—recommending them to the care of local officials and also enabling them to procure horses at the staging posts of the imperial postal service that still webbed the Ottoman domains, a decaying relic of a once-effective administration. But this mode of transport had disadvantages: the weight of the *Milordos*'s luggage was limited and he was expected to keep to the post-track and not spend much time observing ruins by the way. Many travellers, preferring more independent and leisurely progress, hired horses privately, either by the trip or by the day. In the latter case, the owner usually accompanied the party on foot to feed the animals *en route* and take them back home at the completion of the day's march; so while the baggage animals shuffled along in cavalcade at about three miles an hour,* the unencumbered antiquarian could range at will, finding, as he wandered on unpaved thoroughfares, along meadows, through groves and thickets and across mountains, a charm no dusty carriage road could ever afford. If he were sufficiently well-advised to travel in spring or autumn, he would find the ground one gala show of wild flowers, even to the very sides of the path, each group seemingly vying with the other to sport in native bloom all the gaiety of a flower garden. Some visitors preferred to travel by night when the moon was in full splendour; nothing could then be more pleasing or romantic than the winding of the cavalcade among projecting rocks and dismal hollows, when first a gleam of light prevailed and then a solemn darkness veiled and softened all in sweet composure. The glow-worms peeped from the bushes, fireflies glanced in thousands, and how divine the evening star appeared, tipping the dark chain of the mountains! Even her ruins spoke less emphatically of the melancholy fate of Greece than her extensive solitudes; her prodigious plains neglected, her beauteous seas almost without a sail.

Travelling was less idyllic when it came to paying the expenses —a source of considerable irritation to many visitors. In theory,

* Distances were measured on the basis of travel at 3mph; a village was said to be three hours away, ie nine geographical miles; villagers often knew little of the country beyond such a radius and misinformed travellers through mistaken helpfulness or unwillingness to appear ignorant, to the somewhat intolerant fury of the *Milordi*.

a firman absolved the holder from paying for horses, board or lodging. The Turks certainly never loosed their purse-strings and they were in the habit of descending on a village, stripping it of its few provisions and departing without disbursing a piastre, leaving the overtaxed and downtrodden Greek peasantry to bear the cost. Most western travellers refused to burden the villagers in this way, but it took some time for their hosts to learn that the Frank nearly always paid handsomely, with the result that early travellers sometimes suffered from being mistaken for non-paying predators.

On one occasion, when Dodwell was accompanied by some Turks, his party's approach was descried from a distance by villagers who had time to shut up their fowls—almost the only food to be had in Greek villages. In answer to his earnest application for a supply of this kind, they gravely assured him that they had none; even the abbot of the local monastery gave his solemn assurance that not a single bird could be found in a circuit of many miles. The venerable monk had, however, hardly finished his assertion when a treacherous cock within the sacred walls betrayed him by crowing aloud, and was immediately answered by all the cocks in the village. This sudden and unexpected occurrence could not fail to excite unrestrained merriment and, indeed, the circumstance was so ridiculous as to relax the stern features even of the abbot himself. Dodwell was supplied, on his paying double.

All travellers at times suffered from a propensity to peculation and extortion on the part of their suppliers, but so long as all that was involved was a straightforward purchase of food and accommodation, a bargain, however tempestuous, could be struck. It was when the traveller was received in a private dwelling as a guest that the embarrassing problem of presents arose. Though the tradition of hospitality, which the ancient Greeks had considered as so sacred and inviolable, was still partially preserved—and travelling would have been impracticable in Greece if it had not been facilitated by this noble sentiment—it must be admitted that this hospitality was seldom disinterested. It could hardly be otherwise in such a poor country: a parting present was expected, but it was usually a necessity for the host. Some travellers, sad to relate, tended to be overbearing, stifling the pathetic attempts to keep up pretences, regarding everything as their due since they were in effect paying for it, treating their hosts like servants. Presents in kind were bothersome to transport, though Gell armed his party in 1811 with £16-worth of cutlery for the purpose; hard cash was usually acceptable, and when staying at the court of a pasha, his hangers-on would rapidly empty the *Milordos*'s purse.

If the traveller was cheated, however, he would not be abused for protesting against it, though it would have been difficult for him to do so. The existence of modern Greek, known as Romaic, was almost unknown in the West and when encountered on the spot was a source of curious resentment to the collegian, who risked the mortification of having his Homeric Greek mistaken for English by his servant, and to the don who found the ancient place-names altered almost beyond recognition; both seemed to feel that the inhabitants should somehow have preserved the language unchanged for two thousand years. Less demanding visitors found that when the difference between western academic and Greek modern pronunciation was surmounted, the stranger would find much facility in taking up Romaic.

To deal with all these mundane vexations, early travellers were well-advised to hire a janissary, and very able and active the Turk often was, even to the extent of riding behind his *Milordos*'s cavalcade with a long whip to keep his 'troops' in constant motion; for janissaries were accustomed to overawe and cudgel the Greeks into compliance and it was sometimes difficult to restrain their zeal. As the influx of travellers into the Levant grew, the profession of interpreter or dragoman arose, supplementing and later replacing the janissary. These interpreters were reputed to be exceedingly roguish and ready to take advantage, especially of Englishmen, who were thought to have more money than wit; but one Dmitri was an excellent servant to Cockerell and his friends and another remained attached to Stackelberg all his life.

At the root of these travel problems was the fact that many westerners regarded the Greeks with an indifference closely bordering on aversion. Residents like Fauvel and Lusieri dismissed them as nationally and individually depraved; the traveller Tweddell wrote in 1799: 'What do I care about this vile rabble of modern slaves who sully with their ignorance and stupidity this illustrious ground? I make complete abstraction of them.' Ten years later, Cockerell considered their manner to be so disgusting, their whole character so controlled by the Muslim oppression they laboured under, that if it were not for the compassion one felt, they would be really insufferable. Curiously enough, it was left to another detractor, Hobhouse, to admit in 1811 that many were devotedly attached to their country and nation, even to a degree that might appear foolish and incautious, continually expressing their hatred of their Turkish masters and their confidence in themselves; he was also one of the few to realise that they seldom traced their ancestry further back than the Greek emperors and that it was the restoration of Byzantine domination that they wished to see. The Turks, on the other hand, had many western admirers: they were lauded as straightforward, manly and dignified; it was said that their word could be depended upon and that they lived honourable and upright lives according to the tenets of their religion. Only a few observers, like Leake, saw their impassive nobleness as covering a rooted aversion to all European nations and disguising ignorance, idleness and corruption.

Despite all the difficulties and embarrassments, many travellers wandered unmolested through the wildest parts of Greece without a guard and with a quantity of luggage that in southern Italy, or even in more civilised states, would scarcely have escaped pillage. The Philhellene Emerson never asked a favour of a Greek that was not obligingly granted, and in numerous instances he met with extreme civility, kindness and hospitality; other travellers, he admitted, might have been less fortunate, but when they stated the Greeks to be constitutionally unmindful of kindnesses, for what had the Greeks in fact to be grateful? As Byron had written:

Where is the human being that ever conferred a benefit on Greece or Greeks? They are to be grateful to the Turks for their fetters and to the Franks for their broken promises and lying counsels. They are to be grateful to the artist who engraves their ruins and to the antiquary who carries them away; to the traveller whose janissary flogs them and to the scribbler whose journal abuses them. This is the amount of their obligations to foreigners.

MYCENAE AND SPARTA

A tour of the Morea—the Peloponnese—was so popular a venture that there always seemed to be a few English about its routes and at Mistra there was even an 'English Inn' where roast beef and port wine were served.*

The first stop of any consequence was Corinth, some fifteen hours' ride from Athens, though there was little enough to see there: only seven columns remained of the temple of Apollo, four having been recently demolished by the Turkish governor who had blasted them with gunpowder to use the fragments in building a house. Even when they did not blow them up, the Turks utilised ancient materials in a somewhat peculiar way. This was in part because, since their religion forbade representation of the living form, any marbles depicting such subjects had to be employed either face downwards or enveloped in masonry, for instance when paving a bath. Columns were disposed, according to one traveller, with true Turkish taste: some had the capital reversed and bearing the shaft of the column, others had the base where the capital should have been. Antiquarians also complained of the degrading uses to which such remains were put: to prop up the roof of a stable or to dam the stream that turned a miserable mill.

Leaving Corinth to ride south into the Argolid, the conformity of valley and mountain to the description of ancient writers seemed no less surprising than satisfactory, reminding the traveller that the ground he traversed had once been trodden by

* Some 200 travellers, mostly English, have been identified by the author as visiting Greece between 1800 and 1830 (military visitors during the War of Independence excluded).

the heroes and sages of antiquity. Athens began to seem almost an upstart as he neared Mycenae, familiar to him through Homer, not excavation. Climbing the steep slope of the citadel, he would reach the Lion Gate, so choked with rubble and bushes that there was barely space to pass beneath its lintel, the carved lions that stood so proudly on guard covered in the scribbled names of travellers.

The main attraction was the Treasury of Atreus, as the tomb was by then known. This 43ft-high, beehive-shaped chamber, built into an excavation in a hill, had long ago lost the bronze rosettes that once decorated the stone courses of its interior, but many of the holding nails still remained to be removed as souvenirs by travellers, who did not fail to replace them by signatures. The edifice was sometimes put to unexpected use, as when some families whose village had been sacked by a robber band took refuge there from the advancing winter. Settled in groups around the wall, parted from each other by the poor remains of their poverty, by their sacks of maize and their straw beds, they showed, by their apparent diminutiveness, the full grandeur of the edifice; and when the day was closing in, and out of the centre of every cluster the red flames flared against the dead-black dome, the size of the whole was magnified by the dimness, the masses of stone grew more monstrous as they rose, till it seemed that only by the mysterious powers of darkness had this awful cavern been called into existence.

The Elgins, whilst touring the Morea and putting the finger on desirable antiquities, did not fail to inspect the Treasury; the *dromos*—the unroofed approach passage—had been partially cleared by the Governor of Navplion so that their mission could measure and draw, and Lusieri later had a further clearance made, but the net acquisition was only two substantial fragments of the entrance façade.

Then, about 1810, Veli, Pasha of the Morea and son of Ali Pasha of Jannina, took a hand. This Veli was the only Turk of whom it could be said that he had an understanding of the value of antiquarian knowledge or any degree of taste for those models of art which Grecian research had disclosed. Seeing so many curious travellers about his domains, he temporarily became one himself, and on one of his journeys turned aside to visit the ruins at Athens. He pitched his tents outside the city, that no umbrage might be given to the inhabitants, and desired them to consider him as a *Milordos*, come to look at the curiosities of the place. Having thus noted what interested potential clients, and aware of the rumour that valuables were still hidden in the Treasury of Atreus, he searched the interior thoroughly. What he found was later much disputed: some said that he discovered large quantities of gold and silver ornaments, but as he remained notoriously short of cash, this is unlikely; the alternative version, that he found next to nothing for his pains, was supported by the memory of the oldest inhabitants of the near-by village. What is certain is that he gave the Marquess of Sligo two fragments of the columns that had decorated the façade and that were, according to Fauvel and the current ignorance of the Mycenaean style, 'in the Persian or Phoenician taste'. Sligo returned the compliment with a couple of cannons.*

Also recorded is a rumour that Veli found twenty-five colossal statues in the Treasury, but this is probably an echo of his dig near the Roman theatre at Argos, where he unearthed a number, perhaps sixteen, of statues smaller than life-size. He was said by Fauvel to have sold them for £500 to an Englishman, presumably either Gally-Knight or Fazakerley; we do not know what these gentlemen may have done with them, for they presented only one female torso from Athens to the British Museum in 1818 and a votive relief in 1839. Veli also found some gold Roman coins in a near-by tomb and, according to Pouqueville, donated some bronze objects found at Argos to Ali Pasha's doctor. Digging near the village of Meloi on the road from Argos to Tripolis, he dis-

* Sligo's fragments of the Treasury façade went to his seat at Westport, Co Mayo; in 1904, the then Marquess sent particulars to the British Museum; on their being identified, he presented them; two fragments had been donated to the Museum in 1843, yet another in 1900, and all were united with Elgin's fragments into the reconstruction there. Other fragments are at Athens and in various European museums.

covered some twenty-five small columns, presumably abandoning them. Near Mantinea, he found some tombs in which were a few small statues that he disposed of to Sligo. His participation in the Bassae excavations, noticed in Chapter 7, is his only operation undistorted by rumour into guesswork.

Sligo was an almost equally random collector. According to Byron, he had a brig with fifty men who wouldn't work, twelve guns that refused to go off, and sails that cut every wind except a contrary one when they were as willing as could be. Into this precious ark he piled his acquisitions, including a large quantity of vases worth, according to the depreciation of Fauvel, about £8, and shipped them off to Ireland. Byron himself acquired no antiquities: his booty consisted of a shawl and essence of roses for his mother and, for himself, a flask of Attic hemlock, four Athenian skulls dug out of sarcophagi, as many live tortoises, a greyhound that died *en route* and two Greek servants who were quickly repatriated. He did, however, rescue Hobhouse's antiquities, mislaid at Malta.

Neither Sligo nor Veli had exhausted the possibilities of Argos for the antiquity-hunter, for we hear of Colonel de Bosset acquiring two votive reliefs there in 1813 and Leake purchased at least three marbles in the area. Another collector was the naval chaplain Swan, who had difficulty in driving a bargain for a bas-relief discovered when the foundations of a church were being dug. This was beautifully executed, he considered, and he set his heart on securing it, but the Greek proprietor was determined to squeeze as much as he could from Swan's purse; the price quoted varied frequently till at last, believing that Swan had abandoned the struggle, the Greek offered it to a friend of the chaplain's. This gentleman was bargaining for it on Swan's behalf when the chaplain unfortunately arrived on the scene; instantly the Greek refused to complete the transaction and raised the price. Swan left in dudgeon, but in the evening, resolved on a final attempt, he carried the money in his hand in the expectation that either sound or sight of it might seduce the Greek into closing the bargain. But the bas-relief, it was said, had been sold to another Greek for more than Swan had offered. Swan again departed; the Greek followed and proposed conducting him to the person who had bought it. Swan strongly suspected that this was all a trick and determined to see the end. The second Greek, who acted the purchaser, began a long story of his having bought the antique for a friend at Trieste. Swan shrugged and again set forth; again he was followed, with the news that the bas-relief might yet be had, but at an increased price. After long chaffering, Swan carried off the prize for an advance of ten shillings upon the original demand. One suspects that the Greeks had had a thoroughly enjoyable time; it is not known what happened to the bas-relief.

Epidavros was frequently visited. The theatre was comparatively unharmed, even though shrubs had grown up through the limestone blocks of the cavea tiers to spread their green drapery and their golden fringes where once spectators had applauded the works of Euripides. The ruins of the near-by sanctuary of Asclepios, however, had long served as a quarry: the Christians had helped themselves to three Ionic columns, capitals and painted terracotta decorations when constructing a church in Ligurio, and when Navplion had been the residence of the Pasha of the Morea, the Turks had made great use of the materials in the construction and reparation of fortifications, mosques, houses and farms.

Sparta would probably be the traveller's next port of call, and sadly disappointing it was, for of the wealth of monuments enumerated by Pausanias almost the only building remaining above ground was the theatre, and even that had lost its marble. None the less, inscribed stones still lay half-buried in the undergrowth, some of which had suffered from the alarming activities of the Abbé Fourmont, who travelled in Greece by order of Louis XV in 1729. When Dodwell was there, he observed his Greek guide turning over such stones and concealing them; when he inquired the motive for such unusual caution, the guide replied that he did it in order to preserve them, because many years previously a French *Milordos*, after copying a number of inscriptions, had had the letters chiselled out and defaced. It is true that the Abbé not only admitted, but loudly proclaimed that he had committed such vandalism; since, however, he always spoke of the juice of the grape with jubilation, he had probably, as Pouqueville delicately puts it, sacrificed to Bacchus when he wrote to France to say that he had personally supervised the destruction of a number of ancient towns, including Sparta and several others he had never even visited. His reason for so doing was, he said, to ensure that no one should afterwards know where they had stood except himself, this being the only method he could think of to render his journey illustrious. In reality, he may have damaged some marbles in order to acquire the glory of being the only one to have copied them; his somewhat inaccurate reproductions are still extant. It is not surprising, however, to learn that he was recalled suddenly.

One of his more imaginative delineations was a sketch of the Amyclean marbles, votive reliefs then immured in a small and ruinous Greek chapel. He had represented them as carved with human limbs, knives, etc denoting human sacrifice, a practice foreign to the Greeks of classical times. Antiquarians were extremely puzzled by this till later travellers found the marbles to represent articles of female dress and toilet, from slippers to mirrors, a votive offering by a priestess. In 1803, Aberdeen had the marbles removed from the chapel and shipped to England, along with at least three marble heads and some damaged sepulchral reliefs, a fragment of a sarcophagus and various vases and terracottas acquired from unknown sites.

On his travels he had, like other *Milordi*, engaged a tame artist, one Georg Gropius, half German and half Greek, to act as his human camera. When he left for home, he commissioned the artist, subsidising him for the purpose, to acquire and ship antiquities for him, and we know of at least one substantial cargo despatched by Gropius from Malta in September 1808 that included a foot from a Parthenon metope, a torso from Corinth and an altar from Delos, as well as sundry vases, terracottas, bronzes, coins and drawings; Gropius announced further plunder, some of which must have reached England, for the list included a cast now in the British Museum. Except for the drawings, these might have been shipments by Lusieri, but when Byron's major attack on Elgin's depredations and minor sally against Aberdeen were published in *Childe Harold*, Aberdeen was very upset. He had at some stage discontinued his subsidy to the 'Prussian freebooter' and now sent an emissary to convince Byron that Gropius had been making unwarranted depredations in his name. Judging by the quantity of antiquities he had so recently received from Gropius (and, indeed, had removed himself), Byron was too easily swayed when he retracted in the third edition of *Childe Harold*: he now understood, he said, that Gropius had been employed by Aberdeen for the sole purpose of sketching, that gathering antiquities was not in his bond, and that his noble patron disavowed all connection with him except as an artist; if the error in the first two editions of the poem had given Aberdeen a moment's pain, Byron was very sorry for it; Gropius had assumed for years the name of his agent, and though Byron could not much condemn himself for sharing in the mistake of so many, he was happy to be one of the first to be undeceived.

That Aberdeen's conscience was far from easy is also shown by his disingenuous reply to a question from the Committee of Enquiry into the purchase of the Elgin marbles. He had brought home, he said, 'some inscriptions, some fragments; not from the Acropolis but from other parts of Greece'.

The ruins of Sparta had been used in the Middle Ages to construct the near-by hill-town of Mistra; several early visitors, seeing the ancient stones there, believed Mistra to be Sparta, despite classical testimony that the city had been situated in the plain of the river Eurotas. Some even attempted to identify the recorded monuments of Sparta amongst the crumbling Byzantine palaces, monasteries and churches that lined the steep winding lanes of Mistra. Chateaubriand found them positively dangerous: in the quarter destroyed in the Greek revolt of 1770, only fire-blackened walls remained; children, he said, as beastly as the Spartans from whom they were descended, were in the habit of hiding to watch for visitors and push down on them whole walls. Chateaubriand himself was nearly the victim of one of these Spartan games.

Ali Pasha, like his son Veli, appreciated that there was money to be made from excavations. After using the ruins of Nicopolis as a quarry, he decided to dig in them for treasure. Dr Holland accompanied him on a visit of supervision, when Ali, surrounded by his ministers, secretaries and bodyguard, installed himself on a crimson velvet couch placed above an excavation. The doctor could give him no encouragement as to the probable results: the spot was evidently not favourable. Ali soon realised that it was not sufficient to dig at random; one needed informed advice. He therefore pressed Holland with questions as to whether the doctor had discovered any precious metals on his travels, either in the ground or among the ruins he had visited. When Holland explained the improbability, from the nature of the rocks in Ali's pashalik, that gold or silver would be found there, and the equal improbability of there being concealed treasures among any of the ruins, Ali did not appear convinced. Then came the curious circumstance of the loss of Holland's portmanteau containing the papers, journals and maps he had drawn up whilst in northern Greece. The conclusion that Ali helped himself to Holland's papers is inescapable; the likelihood that he derived any benefit from them is remote.

DELPHI

In theory, one of the goals of antiquity-hunters should have been Delphi, but owing to the fact that the village of Kastri, landslides and the rubbish of centuries had covered the temple of Apollo, the treasuries and monuments of his sanctuary, and even the theatre, there was almost nothing visible to acquire. True, the ancient city protruded here and there, and wandering amongst the narrow lanes of the village the traveller might discover a gigantic capital pointing its polished traceries through the weeds that had grown over it, or a fragment of cornice carved as delicately as if it had been an altar. In some places the houses were half new and half old; the lower portions of the walls consisted of ancient masonry, upon which was piled a modern superstructure of pebbles, mud, wood and straw.

Early travellers were unable to reconcile the appearance of the site with the ancient accounts of its splendour, or guess where a town of nearly two miles in circumference could have been placed; this topographical confusion perhaps explains why Byron found the situation of Delphi disappointing, so hidden in a nook as to afford a prospect neither of the profound glen below nor of the frowning precipices above. Yet he and Hobhouse, like Chandler before them, saw one of the main clues to the real site of the temple of Apollo when they were taken into a hovel in the village in which, half underground, was a piece of wall several feet in length and in height, entirely covered with ancient inscriptions; this was, in reality, a portion of the polygonal wall that supports the platform of the temple and was the spot chosen for the commencement of the 1892 excavations by the French Archaeological Mission, who rehoused the villagers of Kastri where the modern village now stands.

Delphi did not, of course, escape uninscribed by travellers. On a column of the north flank of the ancient palaestra of the gymnasium, then the monastery of the Holy Virgin, H. P. Hope and Aberdeen had scratched their names in 1799 and 1803 respectively; Hobhouse and Byron added theirs, and others can still be seen to have followed suit. Hobhouse and Byron were inveterate name-carvers: when they visited the ancient marble quarries of Mount Pentelicon with the novelist Galt, they descended into a small cave by candlelight and, like many who had been there before them, attempted to engrave their names. Galt had no success; Byron did little better; but Hobhouse was making some progress towards immortality when the blade of his knife snapped and cut his finger. So the trio contented themselves with the notable feat of inscribing their initials on the ceiling with the smoke of their candles. They also added their names to the many on the temple at Cape Sunion where an Englishman, perhaps mistaking the temple for that of Venus, had consigned the names of all his 'flames' to a column, closing the list with the words: 'And all the rest of the pretty girls, adieu.'

Such name-carving sometimes had curious consequences, for

Page 103 Cavalcade of Western travellers

Page 104   (above) Temple at Aegina; (below) warrior, pedimental sculpture, in the temple

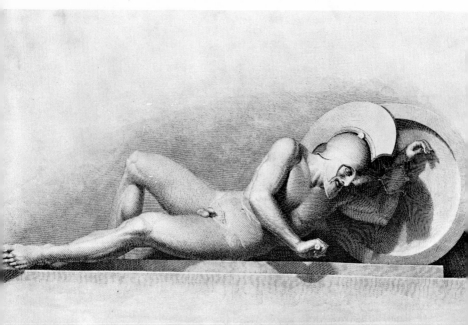

when some travellers visited the Grotto of Pan near Sunion to view its crude and curious sculptures, they found, above the effigy of a headless statue in a chair, the names of Fauvel and Foucherot; these were solemnly and respectfully pointed out by the guide as antique inscriptions. One wonders what would have been made by subsequent travellers of the name-carving accomplished by the Sicilian traveller Scrofani at Delphi's Castalian fountain:

> With the help of a stone which I used as a hammer, I engraved the names of my dear ones on the rocks from which comes out the fountain. I placed in a circle the names of all the members of my family with, in the middle, that of my mother; my uncle immediately after my father, my aunts near my mother; those of my brothers and sisters all mixed up, as they are in my heart. My work was watered by some tears that I let fall, the expression of my happiness at that moment. I then started on my friends' names; all these, interlaced, formed a garland. What pleasure I felt during this delicious work! Praxiteles felt nothing like it sculpting his satyr, nor Phidias creating his Zeus. Twice I tried to engrave my own name between the two garlands, as if to unite them, and twice I abandoned the idea. My name, I am sure, will live as long as my family and my friends; after their death, I would not wish to pass to posterity.

Williams, a Scottish architect, contented himself with making an excavation in the massive foundations opposite the chapel of St Elias near the stadium of Delphi in which he placed a bottle, hermetically sealed, containing separate lists of Scottish poets, poetesses, learned men, his personal friends, and everyone he could think of who had contributed to enlighten his dear Scotland and especially Edinburgh, the fairest among modern cities.

6

AEGINA

When Charles Cockerell viewed the Elgin marbles on their arrival in London, he received a *coup de foudre*. As a budding architect, this induced in him a desire to view whatever examples of Greek artistic achievement still remained in their native setting and to polish his professional attainments by contact with them.

The value of a visit to Italy for aspiring architects and artists had long been recognised and its benefits enjoyed by the *pensionnaires* of the Académie de France in Rome as well as by such Englishmen as the Adam brothers, Soane and Flaxman. A study tour of Greece had been attempted only by Wilkins and by Smirke and Walker in 1802 and 1803 respectively. Cockerell's plan was therefore quite a novel one, but his father, a well-known and well-to-do architect, endorsed it.

The twenty-two-year-old Charles travelled via Constantinople, where he acquired a friend, John Foster, an apprentice architect like himself, a 'most amusing youth' from Liverpool, and a facetious passport from the minister, Stratford Canning, describing him in Italian, the *lingua franca* of the Mediterranean, as of medium height with a triangular visage, black and sparkling eyes, a delicate nose, red mouth, forehead of marble, 'in short, Apollo himself'.

Cockerell and Foster reached Athens in December 1810. They rented a house together, its garden planted with orange trees in full fling and a palm tree so tall as to be conspicuous from afar. They soon encountered a friendly group of brother craftsmen led

106

by Baron Haller von Hallerstein, a Nuremberg architect, at thirty-six the oldest of the group, the other members being Jakob Linckh, a painter from Württemberg, the Estonian Baron Stackelberg, and the Chevalier Brøndsted and G. Koes, both Danes. These five students of antiquity had originally joined forces in Rome, drawn together by a common desire to improve their taste and their aptitude in the arts, till the long-cherished project of Brøndsted and Koes of visiting Greece received the adherence of the other three, and they unanimously decided to explore this new source of inspiration. A meeting so opportune as that with Cockerell and Foster could not fail to promote the object of all their travels by stimulating them mutually in their investigations of the memorable remains that surrounded them. They also had a highly enjoyable time.

Cockerell and Haller became particularly close companions, concluding an offensive and defensive alliance and swearing eternal friendship in the German mode. Haller was not an easy companion, however; he was subject to fits of melancholy, given to moralising which made him as dull as a tombstone, and never thought or talked of any subject other than his studies. Cockerell usually succeeded in laughing him out of his moods and, for his part, Haller had great affection for his young ally; in a memorandum of commissions for Cockerell to execute, he included an item: 'to remain what he has always been for his friend Haller'. The Englishman had larger financial means which, though on the one hand giving him an advantage in the alliance, on the other enabled him to compensate in certain small ways for the benefits he reaped from the German's superior information and science. For Haller's finances were always precarious: he had obtained leave of absence from his Nuremberg post with a £50 salary advance to go to Rome; there he had borrowed £180 from the Bavarian envoy to go to Greece; Cockerell lent him £200 and he borrowed another £180 from a Hamburg friend; but all was eventually repaid. He supplemented his funds by doing views for visitors, partly on Cockerell's recommendation; these included Byron, and Graham who commissioned fifty.

Foster did not take his studies as seriously as these two. Cockerell indeed considered that he idled shamefully and even went so far as to suggest to his father that a hint might be dropped to Foster's parent that better application was required if full benefit was to be derived by the young man from his study tour; Foster's later career was to belie this warning. Foster was also highly susceptible to female charms: though apparently engaged to a fair one in England, he became entangled with a Franco-Polish siren in Constantinople from whom Cockerell rescued him; he finally gave his heart to a charmer in Smyrna whom he married.

Cockerell was more circumspect, though he was long kindly remembered by Félicité Roque, the beautiful and accomplished daughter of a French merchant and cousin to Byron's 'Maid of Athens' and her sisters. These four charming girls, unlike most young Greek ladies, who were kept carefully confined before marriage and even after, were permitted to converse, walk and even flirt with English travellers, and it was considered almost a duty for the gentlemen to fall in love with one of them. There was every opportunity, for if the social life of Athens could not remotely rival the brilliance of the Italian scene, none the less Greeks, Turks and Franks met in a surprisingly constant round of balls, carnivals and visits or, as Byron put it, 'a variety of fooleries with the females of Athens'.

Society was frequently indebted to visitors for evening balls such as the one given by the Honourable Frederick North which was attended by more than ninety residents, forty of them ladies all habited in the Greek fashion, many with great richness of decoration. The dance of the Romaika occupied the greater part of the evening, mixed at intervals with the Albanitiko,* here refined into somewhat less of wildness than belonged to the native dance. Byron gave a supper and dance at the English Consul's

---

* The Romaika was the national dance, employed at religious festivals and performed by men and women together or separately; the chief action devolved on the two leaders, linked by a handkerchief, the others following their movements in a circular outline. The Albanitiko was danced only by men; the leader of the chain would hop quickly forward, then twirl round, dropping frequently on his knee and rebounding with a shout.

house so that two young friends, the Casenove brothers, might see an assembly of Greek ladies. But it was Stackelberg and Brøndsted who determined to give the most brilliant ball of all. Artistic talent was theirs for the asking to help decorate their dwelling, whose galleries and rooms were transformed into magnificent reception saloons by arcades of palm trees lining the walls, festoons and bouquets of fresh yellow roses adorning the walls, and a myriad candles lighting the many-coloured costumes of the guests. When the two friends came to pay the bill, however, they found that their dragoman from Smyrna had absconded with the cash; fortunately, they managed to apprehend him before he had time to spend it and then, not having the heart to turn him over to the brutalities of Turkish justice, let him go free with a stern warning.

Even the Turks entertained at Athens: at a fête given by the Governor, the guests were ushered on to the balcony of his house where musicians were playing and singing an encomium in his honour. Then dancing began in the courtyard below by the light of huge fires of resinous wood; finally, the fires were extinguished and fireworks were played off, the rockets being particularly fine.

The Athenians were occasionally invited to partake of the hospitality of ships of the Levant squadrons of the western powers. When a French frigate put into the Piraeus, the gaiety of her crew was very congenial to the residents, and the Romaika, between French and Greek hilarity, was executed in high perfection. A short time afterwards, an English warship anchored in the harbour; the captain had his lady on board and an entertainment was given to such Athenians as were eligible to be invited; a grateful recollection of this hospitality existed in the minds of the guests, but the preference seemed to be felt towards the manners of the rival nation.

Ceremonious as the westerner found his reception by the Turk, he was seldom aware of how much he involuntarily offended against Ottoman custom and estimate of good manners in his ignorance of the rigid and minute rules of etiquette that governed greetings, seating and conversation. For instance, as sitting cross-legged like the Turks and Greeks was torture to western limbs, the *Milordos* would either perch himself like an Egyptian statue on the edge of the sofa or throw himself lolling backwards with his legs spread out, an attitude scarcely less indecorous than elevating the legs upon the table would be in England. Cockerell and his friends, however, must soon have learnt the rules, for they were on friendly visiting terms with the Governor of Athens, as was Byron; he knew the little band well and joined them in many of their amusements, finding Brøndsted a particularly agreeable companion with whom to tipple punch and talk politics. For there was a good deal of serious drinking as well as decorous participation in the social round; and it is also unlikely that many travellers contented themselves with drawing-room flirtations. Prostitutes certainly plied their trade, despite the almost unanimous silence of visitors on the subject; one does, however, remark that the women of Khrisso, near Delphi, were of a character one would have expected to find near a temple of Venus rather than near the Oracle of Apollo, and Byron's rescue of a 'putana' who was about to be punished by drowning in a sack is well known.

Homosexuality was widely practised in Turkish domains. Ali Pasha's visitors were often embarrassed by the attitudes of his 'pages', and when his son Veli visited Athens he took away a beautiful boy whose mother had to be consoled financially. When the captain of an English ship was rowed ashore in a jolly-boat to visit a Turkish dignitary on one of the islands, the crew was in the charge of a midshipman who so charmed the Turk that he wanted to buy him, making an offer of £200. Cockerell and his friends foiled an attempted seduction at Eleusis; the Turkish *cadi*, under the misapprehension that the *Milordi* treated their Greek lad as their *mignon*, ordered the boy to 'come to him that night'— Cockerell took the precaution even in his diary of writing the phrase in Greek characters. The boy, weeping bitterly, informed his masters; they made strong representations to the *cadi* and left him with disdain. It has been suggested that Byron's relationship with his young protégés, particularly Nicolo Giraud, Lusieri's brother-in-law, was more than that of patron to dependent, but Athenian scandal, which was remarkably well-informed, does not seem to have questioned this friendship.

Despite these distractions, the society of artists worked hard at their architectural studies. Cockerell and Haller would often spend the whole day measuring and sketching, then work late into the night putting their observations into order. Though the main outlines of the monuments in and about the city had already been delineated by Stuart and Revett, by the agents of Elgin and by other visitors, they considered that many details of the greatest importance for the elucidation of the architecture of Greek temples, such as the arrangement and order of their interiors, the mode of executing the masonry, and the ornamental accessories, remained to be discovered and explained. For example, Cockerell and Haller were amongst the first to recognise the use of at least one of the constructional refinements that had been executed with the greatest mathematical precision by the ancient Greek architects: the entasis of the Parthenon columns, that is, a convex curve that replaces a straight diminution of tapered columns. Roman use of this device, sometimes so coarse as to make columns look like cigars, had long been noted: but the subtler Greek mode, a matter of only two inches in the Parthenon, had not. The whole temple, it seemed to Cockerell, far from being a mere superposition of inert blocks of masonry, was alive with movement, and the deviations he found in its construction imparted an effect almost of breathing to the solid marble slabs.*

Though the prime object of the society of artists was the study of antiquity, they were not averse, when this led them to unearth

* There is some dispute as to who was the first to discover Greek entasis. It could have been Wilkins (1802) but it is not mentioned in his 1812 publication. J. S. Stanhope states that at Athens in 1814, his architect, Allason, maintained that he had noticed entasis in columns in the Morea and that this should therefore exist in the Parthenon also, but Cockerell, Haller and Fauvel denied it. Allason fell ill and could not verify the fact, but Cockerell later took the necessary measurements and established the entasis, writing to Allason to say so. Haller, however, in a letter to Cockerell of April 1815 recalls that he and Cockerell had noticed the entasis in 1811 and that Allason was not the first to do so.

examples of it, from profiting handsomely thereby, as we shall shortly see.

Then April and travelling weather arrived. Stackelberg, Brønd-sted and Koes set out for Constantinople: Cockerell and Foster decided to start their tour with the island of Aegina, then three hours' sail from the Piraeus, to explore the famous temple there. Haller shared their interest as did the painter Linckh, a gay youth who had seen much of the world and profited by it—always a commendation with Cockerell. The four agreed to join forces and pool resources.

At the moment of starting, an absurd incident occurred. There had been for some time a smouldering war going on between the Englishmen's servants and their janissary, Mahomet. When the latter heard that he was not to go with the party to Aegina, it broke out into a blaze. He said he was being left behind because the servants had been undermining his character, which they angrily denied. But he was in a fury, went home, got drunk for the first time in seven years, and then came out into the street and fired off his pistols, bawling out that no one but he was the legitimate protector of the *Milordi*. For fear he should hurt some-one, Cockerell went out to him and expostulated, but he was very drunk and professed to love his employers greatly and to be prepared to defend them against six, or seven, or even eight Turks. Cockerell contrived to prevent him from loading his pistols again, and as he worked the wine off, calm was at length restored.

The whole affair delayed the party so long that they did not arrive at the Piraeus till night. As they were sailing out of the port, they overtook the English ship *Hydra*, becalmed with Byron, Lusieri, Nicolo Giraud, and part of the Elgin collection on board, somewhat of an anti-climax, for Byron had given the artists a farewell feast two evenings before and they had seen him off the previous day at the Piraeus. Passing under the ship's stern, Linckh sang a favourite love-song of the poet's, on which, vastly surprised, he looked out of the window of the cabin and invited them all in to drink port and punch till the ship raised sail. Then the island-farers retired to sleep in their small open boat, wrapped in their cloaks, stretched on the bare boards of the deck or the stones of the ballast.

At break of day they reached Aegina, lucky to have arrived un-molested, for the seas around the islands of the archipelago were infested with pirates who preyed on shipping with as much audacity and impunity as they had shown in the days of Homer; pirate boats could often be detected cruising off Cape Sunion, one of their favourite haunts.

The port of Aegina had little to detain the artists. The Vene-tians had shipped away the stone blocks of the ancient harbour to help in the construction of the fortress of Palamidi at Navplion. Almost nothing remained of the temple of Apollo near by; even thirty years before, two columns had stood there supporting an architrave, but by now there was only one, complete with its capital, and three-quarters of another; the former was thrown down by a high wind in 1817, leaving today's lone survivor. The modern town round the port hardly existed; when the danger from pirates had been at its height, most of the inhabitants, numbering some 1,500, had retreated to Palaiokhora, an hour's ride inland, whose scattered remains can be seen on the left-hand side of the road up the mountain. The ruined sanctuary of Aphaea that was the goal of our explorers stood another two hours' ride farther up and was at the time wrongly believed to be the temple dedicated to Pan-Hellenic Zeus.

The myth of Aphaea had a Cretan origin: one of several ver-sions was that, fleeing from the abhorred attentions of Minos, she took ship to Aegina, found refuge in a grove where the temple now stands, and vanished away; she was made a goddess by Artemis and later her identity became merged with that of Athene. Her sanctuary was a most interesting and romantically situated ruin, where the solitude, the imposing aspect of the scattered marbles, the lonely columns and, above all, the view, inspired feelings melancholy yet pleasing. It was conspicuous from the entrance of the Saronic Gulf and from the whole range of the coasts of Attica and Argolis; and when, in ancient times, its polished and coloured front had been lit by the sun, it must have been a landmark useful to, as well as joyfully hailed by the Aeginetan mariner on his homeward voyage as he directed his course amidst the rocks and shoals by which the island was surrounded.

The temple had been erected before the Persian invasion of Greece and was constructed of local limestone, coated in fine marble stucco, with twelve columns on each flank, twenty-one of which were still standing, as well as two at front and rear; inside the cella had been two parallel colonnades (five columns of which were still in place) each carrying on an epistyle a row of smaller columns to support the roof. Despite the damage done by earthquakes, so much was still visible above ground that the friends agreed the temple deserved the most thorough investigation, for it had never been fully measured and delineated, let alone cleared. They decided to establish a camp on the spot for a stay of at least two weeks; Cockerell's tent was pitched for the *Milordi* while the servants and the reprieved janissary were lodged in the cave at the north-east angle of the temple platform.

There was abundance of wild partridges to shoot, and lambs and kids could be bought from the shepherds; fuel was the wild thyme, and when work was over for the day, there was a grand roasting over a blazing fire, in the traditional fashion. The carcass of the whole lamb or kid was rubbed with fat, then sprinkled with herbs and stuffed with almonds, raisins, rice and garlic; when the process of roasting was complete, the spit was propped against a tree to be carved with the greatest precision, the joints being placed on a table formed by branches of myrtle, orange and laurel. The hearts, livers and entrails of the victim were roasted separately on a ramrod and presented to the banqueters before the main course. Knives and forks were used only by the Franks, who complained that the boiled and roast were always done to rags to suit the taste and convenience of a people who eat with their fingers, each man tearing off his portion with his right hand only, for his left was supposed to be employed on services that rendered it unfit for gastronomical use. Easier to manage were the *dolmades* made from chopped mutton rolled up in vine leaves with rice highly seasoned, and a large thin pasty of fowl or of spinach sprinkled with sugar. The milk was chiefly that of the ewe, preferred as yoghourt; cows were kept for breeding purposes and their milk was regarded as unhealthy; the butter, almost always in a liquefied state, looked like white honey; it was kept in goatskins and was very strong, giving a rank and nauseous taste to the rice pillau. The cheese, made of goat's or ewe's milk, was extremely salt, but egg and lemon were even then regarded as desirable additions to soup and sauce.

Fish was readily available owing to the extraordinary number of lean days in the Greek religious calendar. Red and grey mullet, squid and eels were plentiful; snails, cooked with a quantity of garlic, were eaten with high relish, at least by the Greeks; botargo, made from the dried roe of the white mullet, was a delicacy, as was the caviar imported in barrels and looking rather like black soap; it was eaten with oil and vinegar and its fishy taste was not agreeable to all foreigners.

Sweet dishes were very popular, though the pastry was heavier in Greece than elsewhere from the oil used in making the paste and from honey being substituted for sugar; the cakes of the country were indeed a sort of lead to any stomachs but those of Greeks and Turks. Fresh fruit and vegetables abounded, at least in the towns, from peaches and pomegranates to cauliflowers and carrots.

The wine, except that from the islands, was almost invariably resinated, as much as $2\frac{3}{4}$lb of resin being infused into a barrel of 24 gallons. Some travellers managed to overcome by habit the repugnance they at first felt for it; others found it so pungent that they were obliged to substitute raki, the fiery spirit extracted from the stalks of vines taken from the wine presses. Muslims were, of course, forbidden from taking strong drink, though this did not deter a good many whom visitors encountered. The usual Ottoman drink was sherbet, qualified as a very poor liquor, being only sweet water sometimes coloured with marigold flowers and with a few blanched almonds swimming on top. Coffee, then as now, was the most popular of all.

The society of architects soon recognised the need to recruit local labour to help them in clearing the temple and the call went out for volunteers from the near-by villages, whose inhabitants were only too ready to earn the unexpected increment of a wage, for they were mostly tenant farmers, paying their rent in grain, and when the harvest was bad they could be left with none for themselves. But as news of the digging spread, more than were wanted began to congregate around and gave Cockerell a good deal of trouble. 'Greek workmen,' he wrote, 'have pretty ways. They bring you bunches of roses in the morning, with graceful wishes for your good health; but they can be uncommonly insolent when there is no janissary to keep them in order.' One day, in the absence of the janissary, Cockerell had the greatest pother with them, a number he did not want to employ being about the diggings, now and then taking a hand but generally interfering with those who were labouring, thus preventing any orderly and businesslike work. At last he had to speak to them; he said that only ten men were required who would each receive one shilling per day, and that that was all he had to spend; if more than ten chose to work, there would still be only the ten shillings to divide amongst them. They must settle amongst themselves what they wished to do. Upon this, wrote Cockerell indignantly, what did the idlers do? One of them produced a lute, they settled into a ring and prepared to dance. This was more than he could put up with: no work would get done at all. He stopped the entertainment, declaring that only those who worked, and worked hard, would be paid anything whatever. This threat was made more efficacious by his evident anger, and gradually the superfluous men left the workers in peace.

In the account of the excavations that Cockerell published many years later, he described the atmosphere as being rather more idyllic. 'The villagers proved at once their hospitality and their interest in the labours by the readiness with which they assisted the excavations, lightening our toil with the rustic lyre, the song and the dance—now, as in former days, the constant accompaniment of all combined operations in such countries.'

Travelling Franks, however, neither admired nor understood modern Greek or Turkish music. Dodwell ranked the Greek habit of constantly singing to be among the worst of the petty vexations of a journey for *Milordi*, for they were sometimes tormented in this manner by their attendants from sunrise to sunset. When he set out to tour the Morea, he was accompanied by some Athenians with whom one indispensable condition of their employment was that they should never sing. Dodwell was confident that they regarded his want of taste with feelings of commiseration and contempt; and one of his intended servants actually gave up his place from a conviction that he would not be able to adhere to the agreement. Even those who did go seemed incapable of maintaining their promised silence after the first day. Another Englishman, wishing to celebrate his king's birthday in the most public manner possible, hired the Turkish band of Athens to play for him, but was forced to leave his house to escape the noise. The Athenians themselves invariably hired this band to play over the three days of Easter, paying large sums for the privilege including the governor's £5 commission.

A Greek could seldom sing without dancing at the same time, and the rest of the company present could rarely resist the temptation of joining in, as if actuated by a natural impulse. At Athens, on the first of May, there was not a door that was not crowned with a garland, and the youth of both sexes, with the elasticity of spirits so characteristic of a Greek, forgot, or braved, their Turkish masters while, with guitars in their hands and crowns upon their heads, they danced in honour of the May. On Mykonos, some travellers were passing a house when a plate came flying out through a window. 'Pray, what is the meaning of this?' inquired one of them of his servant. 'Is it a mad-house?' 'For Bacchanalians only, sir,' replied the man, going on to explain that it was the abode of a rich man who was making merry with his friends and that it was the custom for the host to break plates as a proof of his magnificence.

DISCOVERY AT THE TEMPLE

The clearing operations, without which it would have been impossible to make measured drawings, proceeded apace. The temple stood on an extensive artificial terrace that had become covered in earth and on which was growing a crop of barley; Greek peasants were apt so to utilise any level pieces of ground, thus saving themselves the heavy labour of terracing their mountainsides. Sizeable bushes and even small pines and cypresses flourished in the ruined interior of the temple, but once these had been removed the architects delightedly realised that it would be possible to find and examine all the stones necessary for a complete architectural analysis and theoretical restoration of the archaic temple and to learn all that students could wish to know of its construction, from the stylobate to the tiles. Haller and Foster were responsible for the plan of the edifice, Cockerell for drawing and measuring the detail, while Linckh busied himself with the general views. Interesting particularities soon became evident, early examples of those refinements that were to characterise the best Greek buildings; for instance, the corner columns were slightly thickened, since otherwise, thought Cockerell, outlined against the unobstructed air that seemed to eat away their substance, they would have appeared more slender than their fellows.

Then a startling incident occurred. One of the party, digging in the interior portico at the east end, struck on a piece of Parian marble which, as the building itself was of limestone, arrested his attention. It turned out to be the head of a helmeted warrior lying with the face turned upwards, and as the features came out by degrees, the four young men were wrought to a high state of rapture and excitement. Here was an altogether new interest which set them to work with a will. Soon another head was turned up, then a leg and a foot, and finally, to make a long story short, they found under the fallen portions of the tympanum and the cornice of the eastern and western pediments no less than sixteen statues and thirteen heads, arms, legs, etc, all in the highest preservation, representing the heroic struggles for Troy. It was evident that the sculptures had been brought down by an earthquake with the pediment on top of them and had all been broken in the fall.

After only four days' work, so much had been dug up that the news of the finds was in every mouth on the island. Linckh pointed out that it was not to be expected that the party would be allowed to carry away what they had found without opposition, which elicited from Cockerell the observation that however much people may neglect their own possessions, as soon as they see them coveted by others, they begin to value them. Linckh, however, counselled practical measures: a boat was sent for to remove all that had so far been found, the rendezvous being arranged at the near-by small port, today's Ayia Marina; with the aid of twenty men and six donkeys, the finds to date were transported down the mountain and embarked with Linckh and Foster as escorts. They slipped quietly into the mainland harbour at Phaleron, hoping to avoid any notice being taken of their treasure, but a Turkish customs officer soon arrived from the near-by Piraeus, shouting in a fury that the boat had been beached in a forbidden area. Linckh countered with an equally furious demeanour, stating curtly that, as a foreigner, he had not been aware that landing was forbidden at Phaleron. The Turk was unable to see what was in the boat and made off muttering. Foster, who had gone in search of transport, returned with an adequate train: the young men bestrode two donkeys, the panniers of others received the fragments, and the torsos were roped to the horses. They delayed their departure till nightfall to avoid exciting attention, reaching Athens at midnight, where they unloaded the precious cargo at Foster's house and fell into bed.

Early next morning, Sunday, Linckh hurried to Fauvel's house to inform him of the party's great good fortune and invite him to view the marbles. He was, says Linckh, astounded by the beautiful work and immediately decided to accompany the two artists back to Aegina. The English consul Logotheti and the French merchant Roque arrived soon afterwards, and Linckh realised that if the find were to be kept safe from the Turks it must be dispersed at once: he took possession of two torsos, two more were transported to Fauvel's house, and Foster kept the rest.

With Fauvel now one of the party, they left for Aegina at two o'clock on the Monday morning, reaching Ayia Marina at seven. Cockerell met them with good news of the latest finds, but also to recount that trouble had been experienced with the islanders. The elders had come to the site in a body and read a statement drawn up by the Council of Aegina in which they begged the *Milordi* to desist from their operations; they feared the vengeance of their Turkish overlord—the Capitan Pasha or Lord High Admiral—should he hear that anything had been removed from his fief without authorisation; furthermore, heaven alone knew what misfortunes might not fall on the island in general, and the immediately surrounding land in particular, if digging was continued. Cockerell was very angry, asserting that such a rubbishy pretence of superstitious fear was obviously a mere excuse to extort money. This comment naturally did not appear in his published account of the excavation, but it seems extraordinary to have begrudged payment when the profit from the sale of the marbles could be expected to be substantial.

The council meeting of the society decided, however, that it was only fair to pay something, particularly since the demands of the islanders had come down from £500 to £50. Linckh, who had £25 on him, gave them to Cockerell's Greek servant, Dmitri, instructing him to offer this sum and only to raise the ante to £50 if there was no alternative. Dmitri managed the affair well and succeeded in buying title to the antiquities already found and removed and to any that might still be unearthed, with permission to continue digging till the whole site had been explored, all for £40. He brought back a receipt for the £25 Linckh had given him, but out of respect for his master had only written the names of Cockerell and Foster on it.

Now the evil eye that was to bedevil the sale of the marbles got to work. Linckh insisted that the receipt must be rectified to include Haller's and his names, since otherwise their title to a part share in the marbles could be contested. But this was easier commanded than achieved. Linckh went down to the village with Dmitri to pay the outstanding balance of the £40 and to hand over to the two local officials the £1 it had been understood each should receive for his trouble. He had been determined not to pay anything until he got a receipt in quadruplicate, but, imprudently, he let himself be persuaded to have a meal and a nap while the receipting was going on. When he got back to the office, he found it closed and discovered that the officials had gone to a vineyard where they were celebrating the windfall. Linckh was very apprehensive by now; he followed them, but they were, or perhaps merely pretended to be, half-drunk, inviting all and sundry to join them in their pleasures without thought of business. Linckh stood firm, however, and refused to leave without his receipts. Eventually, he and Dmitri got the oldest official back to the office, but even here the old man tried to get out of handing over the receipts, raising all kinds of difficulties. Linckh could hardly contain himself, but Dmitri remained calm, and with unlimited patience and by dangling the physical bait of the agreed supplement of £1, which had to be increased to £1 10s, he at last extracted the receipts.

This is to anticipate the outcome, for in the meantime Linckh had spent a day that was among the most unhappy of his life: he had found himself deceived in Cockerell, whom he had thought to be his friend, and even Fauvel had made a wounding remark. Linckh does not explain the cause of the quarrel; one can only assume that it had some connection with his determination to get the receipt altered. Another quarrel had also taken place. Fauvel had brought two workmen with him from Athens and announced that he would like to do a little excavating on his own account. Relying on his discretion, the friends raised no objections until they discovered, to their amazement, that he had appropriated two of their workmen in addition to his own and was digging precisely where the society had just made their most excellent finds. They could not accept this and told him so, in no uncertain terms. The Frenchman flew into a rage and stumped off to measure, in the most superficial manner, what Cockerell and Haller had already measured with the greatest care. However, it all seems to have been smoothed over and Linckh was soon admitting that he had perhaps judged Fauvel too harshly and rejoicing that they were friends again.

Linckh continued to act as transport supervisor for the expedition, ferrying the finds across to Phaleron and hauling them to Athens by night for concealment in the houses of the society and Fauvel. Judicious bribery was employed to ensure safe passage past the Turkish customs post.

Social occasions now interrupted the society's labours. A Turkish tax-collector had arrived on his annual visit, though he appears to have raised no objection to the sale of the antiquities of which he was a witness; he was, in fact, on convivial terms with the local officials. It has to be remembered, however, that the political situation in the islands was very different from that of the mainland, as was demonstrated in the case of Dodwell's janissary. This Turk was highly offended at the air of independence assumed by the Greeks of the island of Poros and felt particularly shocked at their wearing arms and coloured slippers like Muslims. It was extremely amusing to Dodwell to observe the contest between prudence and indignation that was evidently working in Ibrahim's soul: he could no longer indulge himself in his usual ejaculations of 'pig' and 'dog', but was compelled to submit to similar derogatory epithets from those whom he had been accustomed from infancy to consider as slaves. Dodwell's discomfort at the inhospitable treatment that even he received on this island was compensated by the retributive justice which thus overwhelmed Ibrahim.

Aegina's tax-collector was determined to visit the artists at the temple. He arrived somewhat drunk and got drunker over dinner, paying the society the compliment of quaffing their healths while firing off a pistol; Cockerell felt himself obliged to return the courtesy. Next day, the Turk invited the whole party back to the village to sup with him. He received them in a coat covered with gold coins worth £50 and, to the annoyance of Linckh, included in the party the roguish gentleman who had given so much trouble over the receipts. The meal consisted of the usual whole lamb and the evening concluded with the Albanian dance. Poor Haller must have found the proceedings highly uncongenial, not only in view of his serious disposition, but because he suffered throughout the expedition from both toothache and a headache.

It had taken sixteen days of hard work to uncover and remove all the shattered statues, for besides watching, directing and generally managing the workmen, the artists had to do a good deal of digging and handling of the marbles themselves, taking all heads and specially delicate parts out of the ground for fear of the workmen ruining them.* A German traveller was told some years later by one of the workmen that when the Athene of the west pediment came to light, an unspecified member of the society was so overjoyed that he embraced her, took her to his tent, and for a week treated her as his wife, sharing the same bed.

The party had a dreadful journey back to Athens: thunderstorms mounted up, one on each side of them; the wind rose stronger and stronger till all was black as night over the mainland, with incessant thunder and lightning. The boat's captain was unable to get the sails down, for they were wet with rain and unmanageable in the high wind; then the helmsman lost his head and left his post; even when the ship was got under control she was still in great danger, being close to Salamis amongst dangerous reefs, and the party navigated with their hearts in their mouths till they got to the Piraeus. They were still not out of trouble: the storm had caused widespread flooding on the way up to Athens; men and cattle had been drowned and mud blocked the paths. Only with great difficulty did they eventually reach the town.

They were soon hard at work fitting together the broken pieces of their statues, having rented a house as a workshop. Some of the

---

* Also discovered was a single ivory eye, probably from the statue of the goddess that had stood within the cella. The society missed an important find: in 1903, a German expedition discovered the buried and unexplained remains of a third set of pedimental sculptures.

figures were comparatively easy to make whole, and had a magnificent effect in their bold attitudes of combat. The visitors permitted to view them were almost dying of jealousy; by general consensus, they were judged as not inferior to the remains of the Parthenon and certainly only in the second rank after the Belvedere Apollo and the Laocoon, still regarded as the supreme examples of classical art. Fauvel was permitted to make casts of several figures to adorn his 'museum'; he was, naturally, a good deal disappointed that the glory of such a discovery should not be his, though it is difficult to see what had prevented him, instead of opening tombs on Aegina, from clearing the temple himself.

There was one interesting, even embarrassing, peculiarity about the statues: they had obviously been highly coloured. Though the original vividness of the tints had faded on exposure to the atmosphere, there was no doubt that Athene, for instance, had been given brown hair and blue eyes with a red-bordered dress. Not only that: the temple itself had been stuccoed and painted: the background to the pediments had been bright blue and the pavement red. Such circumstances had been noted before: the Parthenon frieze slab acquired by Fauvel had shown traces of colour till these were removed during restoration and the frieze of the Theseion had borne similar evidence. These incontrovertible facts were really very awkward, for they gave a strange contradiction to all the cherished notions of the day concerning the purity of Grecian taste; to connoisseurs, statues appeared more beautiful in their nakedness than they would have done if beheld as originally finished: painted, gilded and invested with metal ornaments and accessories. There was great reluctance to accept the evidence and Fauvel complained bitterly when scholars refused to believe even that funerary bas-reliefs had been coloured. Attempts were then made to excuse the Greeks: unable to credit that the architects of the best period would have carefully selected the purest materials in the prospect of their concealment by a mask of colours, it was hoped that the practice had arisen only at a late day, during the admitted decadence of Greek taste. Even that hope was finally dashed and it had to be admitted that the classical Greeks had not only decorated their marbles, but had given coloured eyes, lips and nipples to their bronzes and reserved their highest admiration for statues of gold and ivory.

EXPORT TO MALTA

Now began the machinations over the sale of the marbles. It was obvious to Fauvel at least that the finding of this treasure was going to try every character concerned—perhaps the quarrel on the island had alerted him. For fear that this should operate to the prejudice of the collection, on which the wily consul himself had designs, he proposed that the four owners should sign a contract of honour that no one should take any measures to sell or divide it without the consent of the other three. This was done, for they all realised that it formed a whole which a king or a great noble-man who had the arts of his country at heart should spare no effort to secure. Haller informed the Bavarian envoy in Rome and Prince Ludwig that the collection was for sale, while Cockerell wrote likewise to the English embassy at Constantinople as well as to his Foreign Secretary; Linckh urged his government to purchase and Fauvel sent an illustrated account to Paris.

Cockerell hoped at first that Sligo would make an offer. 'But the Germans,' he wrote, 'who calculate by the price of marbles in Rome, have named such a monstrous figure that it has frightened him. They talk of from £6,000 to £8,000.' They were not far out.

Next, those wealthy English visitors Gally-Knight and Faza-kerley made an offer to buy out the Germans' shares for £2,000 and, in conjunction with Foster and Cockerell, who were ready to renounce their profit, present the whole to the British Museum. The offer could not be accepted as it did not come up to the price expected by the Germans, nor did it meet their desire to provide their own countrymen with an opportunity to secure the collec-tion. It was finally decided that the only fair way was to sell by public auction; but to do this, the statues had first to be smuggled out of Greece for fear the Turks should either claim them or put difficulties similar to those encountered by Lusieri in the way of exporting them. The English consul was greatly embarrassed when his opinion was sought on the best method of removal, and recommended either a moonlight flit or bribery.

It was now that Gropius was brought in to lend assistance. We have already met him as the agent of Aberdeen, with whom he was still on good terms, for Cockerell had been the bearer of friendly messages from his lordship. Cockerell and Gropius had become great cronies, and the other artists all knew and liked him. He had failed in an attempt to supplant Logotheti as English agent at Athens but had obtained the vice-consulship at Trichery, subordinate to the Salonika post but a busy trading centre.

In concert with Gropius, the society decided to transport the collection to one of the Ionian Islands, Zante, which had been under English protection since 1809 and was the nearest place of security. The statues were dismantled into their fragmented state, wrapped in sacking and roped to the backs of mules, donkeys and horses; the first batch was smuggled off at night to make the long journey to a small port on the Gulf of Corinth; Cockerell followed two days later with the remainder and great was his relief when he reached the rendezvous to find the first consignment laid out on the beach ready for shipment. By good fortune, a ship was lying idle in the bay and the society was able to hire her for the sea passage to Zante. They sailed along prosperously till, towards evening, they heard the sound of firing ahead. Their first idea was pirates and, presently coming up with a large ship which summoned them to heave to, they were rather anxious. But the ship turned out to be a Zantiote merchantman that had shortly before been attacked by four boats demanding to examine her cargo in the name of the despot Ali Pasha. The captain had refused to submit and, when asked what his cargo consisted of, had replied 'bullets'. When he understood there were four *Milordi* on the artists' boat, he begged pardon for detaining them and let them go.

At Zante, the British agent, Foresti, was waiting to welcome them, providing a room in his house in which the marbles could be viewed with advantage before the auction. The commanding officer, General Airey, and his family were also extremely hospitable.

The friends now formally appointed Gropius as their agent with power of attorney for the sale of the marbles. His first task was to advertise the conditions of the sale in the gazettes of the West. The reserve price was set at £6,000, a quarter of which was to be paid cash down; the buyer must undertake to supply each of the four proprietors with a set of plaster casts of the statues; all communications were to be addressed to Gropius at Trichery; the sale would take place on 1 November 1812, eighteen months later.

Cockerell found a nasty surprise awaiting him in Athens in letters detailing the measures taken in England to buy the marbles. His father had taken the bit between his teeth and approached the Prince Regent, who had given orders that £6,000 and free transport and customs entry (worth perhaps £2,000) should be offered for the collection, subject to his approval on seeing it, and that a warship should be sent to fetch it; the ship might be expected at once. Cockerell now realised that he had led the Government, quite unintentionally, to suppose that they had only to send for the marbles to secure them; so when he received a message that Captain Percival in the brig-of-war *Pauline* had docked at the Piraeus, he was in an awkward position. With Haller and Linckh he set out for the harbour in torrential rain; there, to his consternation, lay not one, but two big ships, the *Pauline* and a transport, come on a bootless quest, for which he was in a way answerable.

Captain Percival had already called at Zante, but had been refused permission to embark the marbles and had now come to Athens to seek the authorisation of the proprietors. When he understood the position, he was at first very indignant, not unnaturally, but once he had done his duty in this respect, he settled down to discuss the possibility of removing the statues from Zante, which was in imminent danger of attack by the French, to Malta, which offered safer asylum. Only with great difficulty were Haller and Linckh convinced that this was the best course of action: they considered themselves bound by the advertised sale at Zante and probably suspected that, should the marbles reach Malta, they would be that much nearer the grasp of the Prince Regent; this was indeed a consideration for Captain Percival, who was somewhat of an antiquarian himself, possessing the best collection of silver coins that Cockerell had yet seen. Agreement to remove was finally reached, however, and the captain invited the three friends to dine; ale and porter, which Cockerell had not tasted for so long, seemed delicious and he drank so much that when he went aboard his party's Greek ship to bed, he slept like a stone till the morning drum on the *Pauline* woke him.

Captain Percival not only undertook to transport the statues to Malta; he also consented to take on board two large cases of marbles for Elgin, as well as some belongings of North. He was not popular when he reached England with this substitute cargo.

Meanwhile, the society had dispersed. Cockerell and Foster were off on their travels again, while Linckh engaged in archaeological pursuits about Greece and the islands with Brøndsted. The conscientious Haller visited Zante to supervise the loading of the statues, but his principal interest was now the implementation of the flattering commission he had received from the Crown Prince of Bavaria.

It is now that Prince Ludwig enters the scene as successor to Choiseul-Gouffier and Elgin in the role of collector-patron, appointing Haller as his agent to tread in the footsteps of Fauvel and Lusieri. Haller was invited to purchase and excavate for antiquities, with credits of £700 for the first and £400 for the second. One of the prince's first suggestions was the acquisition of the remaining horses' heads from the Parthenon east pediment; he withdrew on learning from Haller that these were too damaged to be worth removing. Another proposal was the acquisition of two caryatids from the Erechtheion; the porch was, he thought, incomplete since Lusieri's removal of one lady, so the removal of two more would not much worsen matters; the idea was dropped in the face of Haller's protests. Instead, Haller attacked the many still-unopened graves at Athens, and excavated *inter alia* at Ithaca and Megara, producing a slow trickle of finds; in 1816, he purchased the Hellenistic theatre on the island of Melos for £20 and a quarter share for the ex-proprietor of the value of any finds. True to tradition, the prince tried to get firmans for excavating in the Morea, but his efforts were fruitless; he was also disappointed in his bid to purchase the Elgin marbles, should Parliament refuse to do so, but he bought elsewhere with discrimination; it was eventually due to him that the new Munich Glyptothek, though it could not rival the marbles of the British Museum, took precedence over the Louvre.

SALE AT ZANTE

The French were taking an active interest in the Aegina marbles. Fauvel, whilst considering that they belonged to an early style that he called the 'hyperantique' and that they had neither the grace nor the correctness of the school of Phidias, had timidly praised them and sent sketches to Paris. But Visconti, the Keeper of Antiquities at the Louvre, at once recognised their significance; sculpture of that early period was poorly represented in the Musée Napoléon and he strongly recommended the purchase of such outstanding examples of Archaic art. However, with the English in command of the Mediterranean, it would be a risky and expensive enterprise to transport the collection to French soil; the final French offer was £6,000, £400 payable on completion of the purchase, the rest on delivery at Marseilles, transport to be at the risk and charge of the vendors.

Gropius was by now, the summer of 1812, excavating the temple at Bassae with Haller, Linckh, Foster and Stackelberg, as we shall see in the next chapter. Fauvel wrote to him there making the offer, which was considered very handsome by the proprietors; Gropius replied that he had taken note of it and that if he received no better offer by the date fixed for the auction, the statues would be knocked down to the French. He added, however, that the freight, insurance, etc from Malta to Marseilles would cost about £1,250 and that the effective price must be regarded as reduced by this amount.

The English had by no means given up the fight. They had sent the Keeper of Antiquities of the British Museum, Taylor Combe, to Malta with full powers and ample funds to buy. He reached the island in good time, but having understood from McGill, who was the agent for Gropius, that the sale would take place in Malta where the marbles were, and that Gropius himself would come or would send instructions, took it for granted that McGill knew what he was talking about and stayed put, waiting for the auction to take place. Gropius apparently intended at some stage to hold the sale there, for when informing Fauvel of the conditions for the auction, he stated that although these had been drawn up for a sale at Zante, they remained valid for Malta. On the other hand, though Cockerell had written repeatedly to him urging him to advertise that the marbles had been removed to Malta and would be sold there, he never did so. Be that as it may, while Taylor Combe was detained at Malta, the sale came off at Zante, and for a lesser sum than the Englishman had been commissioned to pay.

Gropius's motive in failing to keep Malta informed of the place of sale is difficult to unravel. None of the party seems to have been aware that the English intended to follow up the Prince Regent's offer for, unlike the French, they put in no written bid in advance, and McGill did not inform Gropius of Taylor Combe's presence at Malta. Gropius may have failed through sheer laziness and inefficiency. Another possible reason is that the English were the only buyers from whom he could not expect to make a profit by arranging transport from Malta to final destination; if he could charge such sums as the £1,250 he estimated for shipping them from Malta to Marseilles, he would have made a substantial gain from anyone else.

The successful contender was the artist Martin Wagner, who had been commissioned by the Crown Prince of Bavaria, unbeknown to Haller, to travel to Zante to purchase the marbles. He was nearly too late. By 1 October he had reached French-protected Corfu, but encountered great difficulty in proceeding to British-held Zante; by the 26th, only five days before the sale, he had got as far as the island of Levkas where, since he was travelling on a French passport, he was arrested; however, the commanding officer, General Campbell, knew about the impending auction and was agreeable to providing papers to allow him to proceed. Even then, his ship was overtaken by a terrible storm, a man was washed overboard, and when he struggled into Zante harbour on 29 October he was thrown into quarantine without light, heat or food.

Haller, Linckh, Stackelberg and Brøndsted, all of whom he had known in Rome, arrived with Gropius, a new acquaintance, to rescue him. He was let out, impatiently expecting to view the sculptures, only to learn, to his fury, that they were at Malta. He expressed indignation in the strongest terms that the proprietors, through their advertisements, should have invited the whole world to be present in Zante on 1 November 1812 without bothering to mention that the marbles had been transported elsewhere; such a procedure was nothing less than a swindle, he said. Haller and Linckh tried to excuse themselves by pointing out that it was the English who had insisted on moving the marbles and blaming them for the confusion.

Haller was in an awkward position: he was greatly upset by Wagner's arrival, for not only had his patron prince thus commissioned another to buy the statues, but Wagner had brought an order from the prince requiring Haller to hand over everything he had acquired in implementation of his patron's commission, which was cancelled. Wagner even gave the impression to Haller's friends that the latter had been embezzling the prince's funds.*

Wagner himself was in a dilemma. He was being asked to commit the large credit entrusted to him by Prince Ludwig for the purchase of a collection he was unable to view; he did not feel inclined to risk buying a pig in a poke in this fashion. He knew, however, that his patron wished to acquire the sculptures at all

---

* The probable reason for the prince's action is that Haller's progress reports since his appointment in 1811 had been delayed or lost. All misunderstandings were later cleared up; Haller continued to work for his patron who supplied funds regularly and Wagner's intrigues aborted.

costs, provided they were all they were made out to be. But were they? It was only to be expected that the proprietors would be favourably disposed towards their find, perhaps too much so; but what dreadful remorse would he not feel if he were to lose them through over-caution, if they turned out to be as good as Haller affirmed. Finally, he proposed that since, on the one hand, a decision must be taken that day, and since, on the other, the manifest was not valid as the marbles were not at Zante as stated in the advertisement, a provisional contract of sale should be drawn up assigning the marbles to him, subject to his viewing them, at a price of £6,000. This proposal was accepted by Gropius on behalf of the vendors, since the English had not bid for the reasons we have seen and he apparently considered the French offer as too conditional and in any case lower than that of Wagner once the cost of transport to Marseilles had been deducted.

Wagner agreed that there was no need to go to Malta to view the marbles as he could see Fauvel's casts of them at Athens. He arrived there in December 1812 and found that they exceeded all his expectations: he decided to conclude the bargain and on 30 January 1813 the provisional agreement was ratified, the statues with their appendages were sold to the Prince of Bavaria, and the first instalment, a quarter of the purchase price, was paid to Gropius. Wagner's troubles were not over, however. He had lost faith in Gropius's integrity because of certain confidences that gentleman had made to him concerning not only his earlier life and conduct of affairs in Greece, adventurous to say the least, but also his future plans, even more speculative, now that he had been appointed consul at Trichery. Wagner may have read too much into Gropius's boasting, but it is reported that the merchants of Trichery soon violently opposed themselves to him, either from commercial jealousy or from other causes, and that the grounds of quarrel became so multiplied and personal that the German was compelled to leave and was never able to return.

Wagner now demanded the documents that would enable him to collect the sculptures at Malta and ship them to Rome for restoration. From this moment, he says, arose an extraordinary

reluctance on the part of Gropius to comply, chiefly because that
gentleman hoped, by delaying matters, to force Wagner to conclude a contract with him for transporting the statues, from
which he would have made a handsome profit. He therefore put
every possible obstacle in Wagner's way, till the latter, in a fury,
lodged a protest at the French consulate, declared Gropius responsible for all costs incurred by the delays, and left Athens for
Zante to meet Cockerell.

By this time, Cockerell, having learnt how the marbles had been
sold to Bavaria, feared that his and Foster's zeal for the interests
of their country might seem to lie under an imputation. He at
once set out from Syracuse for Zante, where he was joined by
Linckh and Foster, as well as Wagner. Haller, when asked to join
the projected investigation of Gropius's conduct, refused, appar-
rently unable to believe that a friend could have cheated the
society; he even reproached Cockerell for having written a bitter
letter to Gropius and besought his young friend to be reconciled
with the German, who repented his errors and weaknesses but
who had not failed through spite or any other reprehensible vice.
None the less, on 21 April 1813 a solemn session was held, pre-
sided over by consul Foresti; the lawyers agreed that Gropius had
abused his power of attorney and he was formally deprived of it;
they decided, however, that the Wagner contract could not be
upset. Cockerell thus found himself obliged, in honour and in
law, to abide by the actions of the agent so mistakenly appointed
and a new contract was concluded, cancelling the legalistic tangle
woven in Athens by Gropius.

In England, however, it was still hoped to acquire the statues.
Cockerell senior petitioned the Government to refuse permission
to export the marbles from Malta, demanding a new sale on the
ground of improper procedure in the first and suggesting that
Gropius had been bribed by Wagner to keep the English in the
dark; when he asserted that this bribe was a quarter of the purchase price, he was probably, however, mistaking the first instalment paid to Gropius as agent for a bribe. Taylor Combe
invited McGill to ship the collection to England without further

ado, on the understanding that the co-owners would be paid Bavaria's promised price. In the end, the English had to bow to the inevitable; Prince Ludwig obtained permission to export when visiting London in 1814; Wagner collected the marbles at Malta in July 1815, reaching Rome a month later. The transport cost him £300, less than half Gropius's quotation.

The French were as angry as the English. Fauvel contended that, under the influence of Haller, Gropius had illegally allowed Wagner extra time to take his final decision; had Gropius kept to the published conditions, he would have had to accept the French offer on 1 November 1812. The matter was even submitted to Napoleon, but he had his hands full elsewhere and no formal protest was made.

Payment dragged on for years; Prince Ludwig would not furnish the second and third instalments till he was certain of obtaining possession of the statues, nor the last till they reached Rome; after Gropius's dismissal, payments to Cockerell and Foster were channelled through Haller to Foresti, the last being made in 1817; Haller's death then confused matters and the Englishmen did not receive a final settlement from Foresti till 1820. Linckh received his payments direct in Germany, the last in August 1816. All in all, however, the four co-proprietors had made a good profit: although expenses had been high—warehousing at Malta costing some £350, for example—the outcome had been about £1,250 in each of their pockets.

The Aegina statues were now subjected to a Roman restoration by the Danish sculptor Thorwaldsen, assisted, we are told, by the wisdom and counsel of Wagner. The desirability of making good the missing parts of antique marbles was largely taken for granted at that time; it is arguable that, much as the practice was abused, antiquity would not have had the effect it did on public taste if all had been left mutilated, and many of the statues were not of a quality to be much harmed by the process; all honour is due, however, to Canova for refusing to touch the Parthenon marbles. Cockerell strongly contested the validity of Thorwaldsen's work: heads, helmets and limbs had been supplied without sufficient authority on the basis of arbitrary assumptions; a shield had been placed so that its hollow would have formed a receptacle for rain-water, a ridiculous mistake no Greek sculptor would have made. (These restorations have now been removed.)

Opinion was far from unanimous as to the worth of the marbles. Though aware in theory that Greek art should be classified chronologically, antiquarians had, in practice, seen few Greek originals, let alone examples of Archaic art such as this, in which the bodies of the warriors were executed in a most lifelike style but where no variety of expression on the faces was attempted and all were given the formal Archaic smile, referred to by an Englishman as 'the same stupid smirk on all the countenances'.

But 'taste', then a highly regarded faculty for informed artistic discrimination, was changing. By the time the Aegina statues were placed on view in Munich's new sculpture gallery in 1830, elegance, harmony and delicate grace, those favourite commendations of connoisseurs like R. P. Knight, had been challenged by the strength and energy of acquisitions like the Parthenon marbles; Archaic works were on the upward trend, Hellenistic on the downward. Greek art was coming to be appreciated for what it had really been in all its different periods and manifestations, not as the embodiment of some ideal beauty canonised by theoreticians.

A curious footnote was provided by the German archaeologist Ludwig Ross, who was active in Greece from 1832. Although Pausanias states that the temple of Panhellenic Zeus stood *on* the mountain and although remains of polygonal masonry were seen there, the temple of Aphaea continued to be wrongly identified as that of Zeus, helped by a mystification denounced, in particular, by Ross. A piece of marble bearing an inscription to the Pan-hellenic god was supposed to have been found by the society of artists at the temple site and was published in the third volume of the *Expédition de Morée*; Ross searched for it in vain, till he was informed that it had been faked by the artists in order to mystify Gell, and that when it had become famous, the hoaxers had not dared confess. Ross eventually found it and asserted it was a bad fake; it had again been lost by 1857. It was next thought that the temple had been dedicated to Athene, since she graced the pediment; it was not till 1900 that an inscription was discovered establishing Aphaea as the titular deity.

Page 137 (*left*) Restoration of Temple at Aegina showing pedimental sculpture; (*below left*) Venus de Milo; (*below right*) Athene, metope from Temple of Zeus, Olympia

(*above*) Clearance of temple at Bassae; (*below*) interior of temple at Bassae showing frieze slabs

7

BASSAE

THE RUINED TEMPLE

Pausanias placed the temple of Apollo at Bassae in the first rank of all the temples in the Morea for the beauty of its stone and the symmetry of its proportions. Its existence was almost forgotten in Christian times, standing solitary as it did amongst the lofty and barren mountains of western Arcadia. At some unknown date, an earthquake reduced its interior to a confused jumble, but the ruins were not then plundered in the usual way to provide building materials; there was little temptation to transport such immense masses of stone over the rocky wastes that surrounded the site, even after breaking them into smaller blocks, the process by which so many of the more accessible classical remains had been destroyed.

The first visitor in modern times was a French architect, Joachim Bocher, who was employed in adorning the Venetian-held island of Zante with elegant villas. In 1765, striking inland from the little town of Pyrgos near the Arcadian coast to verify rumours of an ancient building, he came across the ruins of Bassae by chance; but he made a second and fatal visit from which he never returned; it was believed he had been murdered.

Fauvel, Smirke and those indefatigable topographers Gell, Dodwell and Leake were the next visitors, unstinting in their praise of the picturesque site and interesting remains. Then Cockerell, Foster and Haller, after depositing the Aegina marbles at Zante in 1811, decided to return to Athens by way of Bassae.

They journeyed through the lonely glens beyond which rose range above range of mountains, their blue and their purple deepening through the various gradations of aerial distance, the remoter of them shining strongly yet placidly with unyielding snow; for leagues they saw neither human being nor habitation till, one fine August afternoon, they reached Andritzaina, a village near their goal. On the side of a deep declivity, the houses rose one above another amidst gardens and woodland scenery, sheltering beneath the oak, the plane and the cypress. The site presented picturesque attractions so irresistible to artists that the friends stopped to sketch. They had not long been so employed when a troop of young Arcadians came running towards them with baskets of fruit and flowers, offerings of welcome. Thus the scene, says Cockerell, was invested with a moral beauty in addition to the charms with which it was endowed by nature, for everyone seemed to think it the proper thing to show some attention to the strangers. Some of the girls were very pretty and presented their gifts of pears and figs in the most engaging manner.

The dignitaries of Andritzaina tried to frighten the three friends from visiting the temple—the 'Columns' as it was called, and still is locally—with horrendous stories of one Barulli, captain of a company of klephts or robbers who haunted the ruins. Brigands were a very real hazard: Brøndsted was robbed of all his valuables in the Mani, and when Stackelberg was later on his way home, he was taken prisoner by brigands who ransacked his baggage, dragged him over land and sea, and demanded £4,000 ransom, payable within ten days under penalty of loss of a limb, nose, ear, etc at each repetition of the demand and, finally, of life itself; the steadfast Haller rescued him for a ransom of £550.

Undaunted by the threatened peril, the friends set out, unable even to see their goal, screened from view as it was by the precipitous cliffs that rose beside the steep and rocky track, till suddenly, turning round the edge of a bluff, the temple front presented itself within a few paces to their astonished gaze.

They were soon at work, digging, drawing, measuring and

mentally reconstructing the shattered temple in the form designed, according to tradition, by Ictinus, the architect of the Parthenon; Cockerell was convinced he could recognise the hand of this old friend in the columns that so much resembled those of Athens. Soon, however, a local official arrived begging them to desist from digging or moving stones, since this might bring harm to his village from the Turks, who banned all such activities. The artists replied untruthfully that they had firmans allowing them to excavate and promised facetiously that they were not going to carry away any of the columns. They set up camp much as they had done on the island of Aegina, living on the sheep and milk sold to them by the shepherds who stalked about with guns over their shoulders and long pistols at their waists, looking very savage and wild. These shepherds were of Albanian origin, and the presence of settlements of this people throughout Greece was confusing to travellers; some were Muslim, some Christian, nearly all spoke Greek; some lived as shepherds in the mountains when they were not bandits; some, called Arnauts, formed the bodyguards of Turkish pashas; some inhabited the islands, intrepid seamen as at Hydra; and some cultivated the plains of Thessaly, Boeotia, Athens and the Morea.

Then came a repetition of the astonishing discovery at Aegina. In the space inside the columns was a mass of fallen blocks of stone; while the party was scrambling about among these, a fox that had made its home deep down among the stones, disturbed by the unusual noise, got up and ran away. Cockerell ventured down where the fox had come from: a narrow and tortuous passage that he descended head foremost, whilst his companions held him by the legs. At the bottom he discovered the fox's nest —happily then unoccupied—and, on removing this, he could see a sculptured bas-relief: Greeks and centaurs appeared in all their energy to his astounded gaze. Still suspended upside down, he made a rapid sketch of the slab; from the position in which it lay, it could be inferred that the whole frieze that had once decorated the cella walls would probably be found under the dilapidations.

This discovery opened the most interesting prospects, that were almost immediately to be dimmed. First, the labourers deserted as a result of pressure from the local officials; there was nothing for it but for the *Milordi* to do the digging themselves, though it resulted in Cockerell hurting his hand and all fatiguing themselves exceedingly. Then, when they had just lit upon some beautiful caissons fallen from the temple roof, a man on horseback arrived with four armed attendants; he told them that he was the owner of the land and, although he was very civil about it, he forbade them to dig any more.

So many objections had been made to their digging that the friends felt it would be dangerous to continue without securing official permission. Cockerell and Foster rode over to visit the Turkish governor at Phanari, who received them almost too civilly, squeezing their hands tenderly. He was too much a man of the world, said Cockerell, to show any expectation of a present, though when he examined a picture of Foster's with more than ordinary attention, they could not but have their suspicions. Foster could only promise to send a miniature of it, while Cockerell diffidently proffered a bag of Peruvian bark and a portrait of the English king. The Turk appeared delighted and assured them he would take the latter with him to Constantinople so that he might be reminded of his young acquaintances even there. Despite all his civility, however, he was adamant in banning any excavations without express permission from Veli, the Pasha of the Morea (see p 95), for Veli was very emphatic that no permission to dig should be given by anyone but himself and he insisted on knowing all about travellers in his pashalik and on personally inspecting them and their firmans. The Governor added that the mere fact of the party having remained ten days at Bassae was enough to ruin him; despots asked but few questions and listened to no excuses.

So there was nothing for it but to get quickly through what drawings and studies were possible without excavating, cover up the sculptured stones and abandon the lonely mountain retreat. The only trophy was a fragment of the volute of one of the Ionic capitals that Cockerell presented to the British Museum.

PERMISSION FROM THE PASHA

The authorisation of Veli Pasha was essential not only to conduct excavations at Bassae but also to ensure liberty to remove anything that might be found. There was no time to lose, for it was rumoured that Lusieri had got to know of the discovery of the frieze and was planning a descent himself. The society naturally turned to that sharp fellow Gropius (it must be remembered that the dissensions over the sale of the Aegina marbles had not yet arisen). Veli's financial position was becoming precarious: his luxurious and sensual character and the number of troops maintained in his pay had rendered the expense of his court at Tripolis very onerous; in addition, he had to provide more tribute to the Sublime Porte than his predecessors (some £150,000). This had led to his adopting harsh measures for obtaining money from the peasants and he welcomed other sources of income such as the sale of antiquities from his domains. With Gropius's help it was agreed that, in return for half the produce of the dig, he would give the society the necessary permission and also pay half the cost of the excavations. Gropius was made a part-owner in return for his services, as was the English traveller Legh, who made a loan towards the costs though he did not take part in the dig.

Veli duly supplied a firman addressed to the primate of Andritzaina, by which the latter was obliged to supply workmen, tools and food; he also sent representatives to be present during the dig and to ensure that everything was done properly and in accordance with his orders. The excavating party assembled at Andritzaina early in July 1812: Foster, Haller and Linckh; Stackelberg; the Danish antiquarian Brøndstedt and, of course, Gropius. Cockerell was absent, travelling in Sicily.

The order at once went out to the shepherds to present themselves for work at the excavation of the temple; delighted at the prospect of earning an increment to their meagre resources—the wages were to be a shilling a day—they left their flocks in the charge of their old people, wives and children and came to work for the *Milordi* at the Columns. They were not attracted only by the financial rewards, however; they were curious to know what could be hidden in the strange, inviolate place that had always seemed bewitched to them. Stackelberg writes that the name of Hellene still lived amongst them as a designation for all heroes and giants but without any apprehension that they themselves might be the inheritors of such glory. On the contrary, they imagined the Hellenes to be the forefathers of the Franks, the learned strangers who, they believed, had once owned their land. They thus explained to themselves the visits of western travellers and the value the *Milordi* attached to the remains of antiquity.

Living close to nature as they did, the material needs of these shepherds were few; a piece of brown cloth thrown over some branches to make a tent, a milk pan, a few sheep, a dog and a gun for protection, these were enough for a household, though only a slight increase in their poverty was enough to turn them into brigands. In strange contrast to the simplicity of this existence was their taste for rich apparel: the women spent many hours stitching embroidered waistcoats of red, green or purple velvet, and circular silver clasps fastened the broad sash round the waist, in which were stuck pistols and yataghans, richly chased. The top coat was the capote of sheep or goat skin, but the oddest part of their appearance was the hair: they shaved the fore part of the head and were particularly careful to encourage long and flowing locks, thus giving themselves an indescribable air of wildness; a small red skull-cap covered the crown of the head. The importance attached to richness of dress was characteristic of the Turkish dominions and Frankish clothing seemed oddly plain there, if not unsuitable. One party of travellers found that the supposed folly of their attire excited loud and repeated fits of laughter, though the villagers concerned were otherwise very civil. Certainly, the wear and tear of eastern travel wreaked havoc on the modern frock; visitors were apt to find themselves with hardly a rag to their backs and clean shirts on Sundays only.

Since the temple was so far from inhabited places and the track up to it so difficult, the friends decided to take up their abode on the site. And so Camp Francopolis was born. As the tents they had brought with them were not sufficient for the whole party, huts were built from green boughs which, for better protection against the heavy dews and the cold that struck even in the summer nights, were set against the trunks of wide-spreading oaks or anchored against boulders. On the 'main square' of the camp, poles were driven into the ground and pieces of Arcadian cloth draped over to provide a living-dining-room for the *Milordi*; Doric capitals and column drums from the temple served as chairs and tables. A large area was enclosed by leafy branches to form a museum where the works of art found in the excavations could be examined, classified and recorded.

The fame of Camp Francopolis soon spread far and wide. The principal persons of the near-by small towns came visiting and were invariably received according to strict protocol, pipes and coffee being handed round by the young shepherds. Installing themselves on the carpets they had brought with them and continually running their beads through their fingers, they would watch the digging, amazed at the interest taken by the Franks in the stones of the temple. The peasants from all around soon followed this example. As night fell, fires would be lit, over which whole lambs and kids turned on wooden spits, while the generous contributions of Bacchus were proffered, as in antiquity, in a primitive goat skin. Soon the music would begin and then the dancers would come forward to express in their wild leaps and turns their joy in life. Seeing the people assembled there, it was easy to imagine the site as it had been in ancient times, animated by crowds celebrating the periodic festivals of pagan religion with all the solemnities of the choregic dance and the pythian hymn; Apollo himself, roused from his long repose, might have thought that the glorious days of old were about to return.

But it was not all dancing and feasting: there was serious work to be done. Debris rose as high as sixteen feet in the centre of the temple; though only two of the thirty-eight surrounding columns had fallen at the south corner, the west flank had a dangerous tilt outwards, and all four columns of the porches were down.

Sometimes up to 100 shepherds were employed in clearing the site at a time. Musicians lightened the toil with their tunes, giving the signal to start and finish work, accompanying with the lyre the shouts of the workers and the rolling of the temple stones, while the beat of the big drum, doubled by echo, resounded through the mountains. Thus the inspiring aid of music, as necessary to the Greeks at Bassae as to the Hellenes who rebuilt ancient Messene under Epaminondas, was never wanting, though the flutes of antiquity were perhaps ill replaced by the rustic pipes of the new Arcadians.

The workers, in long rows, with ropes and pulleys, were set to drag the fallen blocks of stone out between the still upright columns. The united strength of thirty men was often needed to shift them, for they lay in jumbled and awkward, even dangerous positions. Sometimes the music would abruptly cease; in the sudden hush, a fragment of sculpture would be brought out to join its fellows in the 'museum'. Slowly, block by man-handled block, the pavement of the temple was disclosed; here, thrown down in confused dilapidation, lay the internal columns that had supported the sculptured frieze now equally in fragments amongst them. The interior of the cella had been divided into a small rear chamber to the south, the adyton, and a larger front one; from either side of the latter, five short spur walls had projected towards the centre; these had been erected at right angles to the cella walls except for the two near the adyton, which had been set at an angle of forty-five degrees. The jutting spurs had terminated in columns with Ionic capitals which had carried the frieze running all round the inside of the cella; one column only remained standing, a piece of wall attached to it. An isolated column had divided the main chamber from the adyton; its capital had been of the Corinthian order, the earliest known example; Haller surmised that its two neighbours had also carried Corinthian capitals, for he found fragments similar to those on the extant one that could not otherwise be accounted for. (The 1908 excavations confirmed this.) These three columns had formed a backdrop to an over-life-size bronze statue of Apollo the Succourer, but in

369 BC this had been transferred to Megalopolis and a wood and marble effigy placed in its stead, a few fragments of which were found by the society.

With the greatest care, they loosened and removed even the smallest fragments of worked stone. As they matched breaks and fractures, they were able to piece together whole slabs of the frieze, often from as many as thirty fragments. Watching the component parts fall each into its original place kept the workers' interest continually alert and fresh; almost as the original sculptors had seen the frieze grow under their chisels, so the artists saw it grow by reconstitution till they had nearly the complete run. But though fragments of the Ionic capitals from the inner columns were found wedged between the coffered limestone slabs that had lined the roof over the niches between the spur walls, they were so damaged that reconstitution had to be conjectural. The absence of the clamps and pins that had held the frieze slabs in position showed that the temple had been plundered for metal at some time previously; also, the lone pillar with the Corinthian capital had not simply fallen from its original position but was inexplicably lying quite a distance away.

Outside the temple, some pieces of the six metopes that had decorated each entrance were found lying under the fallen part of the southern architrave; farther beyond, rising ground led the artists to hope that pedimental sculpture similar to that of Aegina might lie buried. Two tall oak trees that seemed like guardians of the temple remains had grown over these mounds, and the society debated at length what to do about them; their huge roots hampered investigation; in the surrounding multitude of trees their loss would hardly be noticed. It was decided they must go.

The earth was first dug out from between their roots; then ropes were wound round one of the trunks and eighty shepherds, shouting mutual encouragement, started to haul. For some time all their efforts were in vain; each time they eased off, the tree settled back like a sacrificial animal unwilling to be dragged to the altar. At last the trunk gave way and its crown of branches, as if borne by a gale-force wind, slowly sank with terrifying loud cracks, breaking up as it touched the ground. The shepherds rejoiced at their victory till a feeling of sorrow came over them as they saw the huge tree lying prostrate. Under the roots were found more broken pieces of metope, as well as the beautiful acroterion that had crowned the temple gable; but great was the disappointment when it was realised that no pedimental sculpture lay concealed. None has, indeed, ever been found, and it is supposed that it had been looted by the Romans.

But these idyllic conditions were not to last long. One evening, when the wages were being shared out by Veli Pasha's overseer, a quarrel broke out over some missing excavating tools. The overseer voiced suspicion of one of the shepherds; the accused threw himself amongst the bystanders to vent his wrath and tried to drive them away with abuse and blows, shouting that everyone was maligning him, then fled into the mountains. Another shepherd, because of his independent attitude, was struck by the servant of the pasha and dared to turn against him. All was confusion: weapons suddenly appeared, a shot was fired, then another; the shrieks and lamentations of the women added to the uproar; soon all was battle, flight and pursuit.

The immediate trouble was glossed over: the shepherds sent a deputation to the Turkish magistrates to pray for forgiveness and the society wrote a strong letter supporting them. The guilty man was found and imprisoned. But the atmosphere had been poisoned and trouble was brewing.

Veli Pasha had been sent regular progress reports of the excavations, but rumour had been at work to change the sculptures of white marble to figures of pure silver and raise his expectations of gain to the highest pitch. Drawings could content him no longer: he wished to see the reality. In response to a peremptory order, half the marbles had to be sent to him at Tripolis, even though the difficulty of transporting them over high and untracked mountains greatly endangered their safety. Despite all the society's care, one piece was lost; however, it was rescued a year later by the traveller J. S. Stanhope from a farmer's cottage. Veli was not pleased with what he saw: mere fragments of marble, discoloured by age. He sent them back with a message expressing his astonishment at their beautiful execution and amazingly life-like representation.

He soon had other matters to occupy him: it became known that he had been the loser in the game of intrigue being played at the Sublime Porte in Constantinople and his deposition was pronounced. The immediate consequence was that robber bands made their appearance in the Morea, intending to profit from the period of unrest that was expected to intervene between the departure of one pasha and the installation of another. The society set a watch each night, a wise precaution as was demonstrated when, in preparation for an attack, spies of a robber band hid themselves unnoticed amongst the fallen columns. The watchman had kept a big fire blazing in the centre of the temple floor; suddenly he noticed two crouching shapes that he had at first mistaken for part of the excavations; then the firelight glinted on a flintlock. He was unarmed, but had the presence of mind to raise his shepherd's staff to his shoulder like a gun and shout an alarm. All rushed out fully armed and the robbers fled, hastened on their way by the bullets of the defenders.

The arrival at Tripolis of an envoy from the Sublime Porte formally summoning Veli Pasha to give up the pashalik of the Morea solved the society's major problem; they had been in a state of great anxiety lest Veli should insist on strict performance of the agreement that, in return for his help, he should receive half of whatever might be discovered, and had foreseen that it would be impossible to convince him of the absurdity of dividing up a series of marbles that owed much of its value to its continuity and completeness. Now, however, superseded in his domain and eager to realise all the cash he could, he demanded £2,000 but accepted the society's offer of £400 as his share of the spoil. Legh and Foster advanced the necessary funds, repayable in bills on London as soon as the Aegina collection had been sold, the marbles being mortgaged as security at 6 per cent interest.

The artists next learned, however, that Veli's enemies were planning to contest his right to the £400 compensation; it was obvious that the sooner the marbles were removed from Turkish jurisdiction the better. They therefore applied to him for the necessary firman as well as an order requiring the shepherds to help in the task, for the local officials had begun to exercise delaying tactics, fearing that the new pasha would vent terrible wrath on the villagers if they allowed the spoil to be removed with no profit for him.

When the documents arrived, preparations for the transport to the coast were complete, with the sculptured fragments wrapped in sacking and wooden cases constructed to hold them. Just when all had been made ready, however, a small conflagration broke out amongst the huts. No one wished to leave a half-burnt happy home behind him: torches were brought and the whole of Camp Francopolis burned to the ground. All trace of those leafy bowers vanished like a dream and the great gaunt form of the temple was left to its lonely vigil and the slow march of time, the pillars sunk with years and fatigue, weary of standing in their wild and wind-swept isolation. The oldest shepherd, the leader of the clan, with patriarchal dignity, wished the Franks 'happy hours' and assured them that at the return of summer the following year he would be thinking of them, and that his children and his children's children would recount the story of how the strangers had come to live amongst them.

And so the caravan departed: 150 men carried the antiquities, six to eight porters barely sufficing to support some of the large pieces. Such was the unevenness of the tracks that every step had to be watched as the procession wound its laborious way through the gorge of Kotilion to reach the river Neda, which it followed down towards the tiny port of Bouzi. Here the party found themselves in a dangerous situation, for the Turks thereabouts had a reputation for exceptional brutality and the Greek officials seized the opportunity to try delaying tactics again, first attempting to conceal part of the works of art, then seeking to raise a revolt amongst the porters and persuade them not to proceed farther. Only with difficulty did the artists succeed in re-establishing order and good relations.

Now came a new danger: the French, who were in possession

at Corfu, were said to be sending a privateer to seize the treasure. Foster went ahead to the British-held island of Zante to enlist the help of the officer commanding, General Airey, who, without ado, ordered him to be supplied with a naval escort. He found the marbles already loaded on to a ship at Bouzi and the convoy set out in good order, but winds and thick fog separated the ships and it was by sheer good fortune that the heavy-laden transport reached a safe harbour at Zante.

According to a story that became current some time later, everything had been loaded with the exception of the Corinthian capital from the temple cella which was still standing half in and half out of the water when the incoming pasha's troops arrived to stop the embarkation; the ship had to put off without the capital, and the artists had the mortification of seeing it hacked to pieces by the furious Turks. This was, in fact, mere imaginative embroidery, for the capital had never been removed from the site, as is proved by the fact that Haller later requested Cockerell, should he visit Bassae again, to re-record the details of the capital. This was because Haller had been nearly shipwrecked and all his drawings of the Bassae temple, in duplicate for himself and Cockerell as was their practice, as well as some antiquities, had had to be thrown overboard to lighten the ship; he still possessed his rough journal, however, and from this was able to reconstitute most of the lost material.

The arrival in Zante of the little band was in one way a sad occasion, for it was here that their friend Koes had died a year before, and they were to stay in the very house where he had breathed his last. He had been buried in the English military cemetery and Brøndsted set up a gravestone with a verse from the *Iliad* inscribed on it.

The frieze slabs were soon displayed to best advantage in a large rented room. But a problem arose: what had been their sequence when erected in the temple? Eleven slabs clearly belonged to the battle of the centaurs and lapiths, twelve to that of the Amazons. Each was a complete picture in itself. So began a recurrent controversy and only today, on the evidence of the holes and cuttings for the dowels and clamps that had held the slabs in position, does it seem that a correct solution may have been reached.

The proprietors were over-enthusiastic about the artistic worth of their discovery, though in times when so few examples of original Greek sculpture were known, they can hardly be blamed. Foster wrote to his father with unfounded optimism that, since the Bassae temple had been erected at much the same time as the Parthenon and by the same architect, Ictinus, Phidias must surely have collaborated in the carving of the Bassae frieze as he had at the Parthenon. If Phidias were indeed the sculptor, Foster went on, he had not done his duty by Athene in Athens, since her marbles were much inferior to those of Bassae in many instances: sculpture in such high relief was unique, some parts of the figures being actually detached from the background; nothing like this new discovery could be seen at Rome or Paris. Brøndsted wrote ecstatic letters from Camp Francopolis to Fauvel, dating them Year I of the resurrection of the Amazons and centaurs and regretting that his friend could not come and share with the society all the benefits that Apollo the Succourer of the Phigalians had deigned to grant the society. Fauvel passed the information on to his minister in Paris, praising the marbles on the basis of some sketches by Gropius. A year later, however, in 1813, he changed his tune: the preliminary drawings, he said, had not enabled him to make a proper assessment; knowing the tradition that Ictinus had designed the temple, he had been too favourably disposed in advance; now that he had seen a more complete representation, he judged the reliefs to be extremely mannered, with floating draperies twisted in an extravagant manner and no facial expressiveness; had not the frieze indubitably formed part of the temple, he would have taken it for Roman work; it had none of that beautiful Greek simplicity, that excellent composition that one saw on the bas-reliefs of Athens. It has to be remembered that, if his government had purchased on his recommendation, he would have been responsible for the expenditure of a large sum of money; little wonder that, in anticipation of the judgements that would be passed in Paris by experts like Visconti, he hesitated and even back-pedalled.

Martin Wagner also hesitated. When purchasing the Aegina marbles at Zante in November 1812, he saw the Bassae frieze; his prince was prepared to offer up to £18,000 if Wagner could assure him that it was of the school of Phidias and could therefore, by implication, rival the Parthenon frieze. Wagner could not. He did, however, make drawings of it that, to Haller's indignation, he published in Rome in 1814 before the owners had been able to profit from their discovery in this way.

Gropius having been dismissed from his functions as agent for the society after the affair of the Aegina marbles, the other co-proprietors took over his duties and each kept his government informed of the arrangements for the auction, which was advertised on their behalf by consul Foresti to take place in Zante on 1 May 1814, some eighteen months after the excavation. All the society were present to ensure a proper sale: Haller, Linckh, Stackelberg, Cockerell, recovered from a bad bout of fever, and Foster with his Smyrna bride and child. Local custom was followed and adjudication delayed till nightfall, marked by the blowing out of a candle. Fauvel, despite his doubts, had carried out instructions from Paris and put in a bid for £8,000, but the marbles were knocked down to the Governor of the Ionian Islands, acting for the Prince Regent, at the reserve price of £15,000 (as a result of unfavourable exchange, £19,000).

Haller was the only one not to benefit. In 1811, he had offered his share to Prince Ludwig, partly because he could not afford his part of the excavation costs, partly to prove his good faith after Wagner's intrigues. Receiving no reply, he borrowed to cover expenses and by 1813 his financial situation was desperate; luckily the prince accepted his offer, sending a credit in the nick of time. Haller was able to meet his obligations, but he forewent the profit of more than £2,000 that each of the other co-proprietors received.

The marbles arrived in England on 12 July 1814. Upon opening one of the cases, a live scorpion was found, but this was not the only stir they caused: connoisseurs were astounded by the swirl of fighting, biting, charging, strangling protagonists depicted. The representation of strong passion or of any kind of mental or bodily exertion was objectionable, they said; where in the frieze was Winckelmann's calm grandeur? Where was ideal beauty? Greek sculpture could never have been like this! What made it worse was that the Bassae frieze, like the Aegina sculptures, had originally been highly coloured: on a background of bright blue, varied tints of purple, red and green had been employed on the vestments of the contenders while their helmets and spears had been of polished metal. The best that could be said was that the frieze was curious, instructive, and an essential document for the history of art; but not beautiful. The belief that it was the work of Phidias remained prevalent, however. When Stanhope arranged for the slab he had rescued in the Morea to join its fellows in the British Museum, Sir Joseph Banks sent his carriage and four to convey it there, wishing to do honour to the famous sculptor.

From then on, the temple at Bassae was constantly visited, drawn and measured, though this did not prevent further depredation of its ruins. One of the villagers from near-by Skliru boasted that during the War of Independence he had thrown down two columns to get at the lead round the metal clamps uniting the drums.

This does not, however, explain the allegations of disgraceful vandalism that were later brought against the excavators who, in the over-heated imaginations of certain anglophobes, became Albion's antiquity-pillaging sons—Foster was, of course, the only Englishman there. Christian Müller was the first to publish, in 1822, a garbled recital of destruction and theft under the protection of armed force, and on this basis Colonel Bory de St Vincent, a fiery member of the 1829 French expedition, produced an even more inaccurate diatribe. Ignoring Bocher's published statement that in 1765 the interior of the temple was completely ruined,

Page 155   Greece today: the Temple at Bassae, Peloponnese

Page 156 Greece today: (*above*) another view of the Temple at Bassae; (*below*) Eleusis

Bory affirmed that the edifice had been intact when discovered by Dodwell in 1812—six years after that gentleman had left Greece—and alleged that the English had torn down the Ionic columns supporting the frieze; thus looted for the benefit of London by a band of speculators, it was condemned to languish under the foggy sky of a smoky city, where few foreign artists were admitted to study it and where only a few inhabitants understood its beauty. This, he went on, was an action similar to the brigandage practised by Elgin at Athens; these two expeditions would always remain characteristic of the English in the history of art, and posterity would know that what no other nation had dared to do, what was even repugnant to the Turks, had been done by the vandal English.

Such derogatory opinions were widely held by the French, for they accused Elgin of destroying the façade of the Monument of Thrasyllos in Athens when it was Turkish shot in the War of Independence that had done the deed. Voutier, a French officer who joined the Greek forces during the war, lent his voice to the chorus of denigration, alleging that the Aegina temple had also remained in fairly good preservation till English cupidity penetrated its solitude and looted its statues. One suspects that had Choiseul-Gouffier been more successful in obtaining Parthenon pieces or Fauvel in purchasing the Aegina or Bassae marbles, these comments would have been different.

Bassae was the last joint enterprise of the society, though Veli, after his appointment to the lesser pashalik of Thessaly, did not abandon his antiquity-hunting and invited them to participate; they declined, pleading prior engagements.

Haller continued his researches on behalf of the royal house of Bavaria. His despatches to Munich included a large marble vase decorated in bas-relief, inscribed marbles and assorted pottery unearthed at Athens; a piece of the Erechtheion decoration, and a Doric capital and some fragments from Aegina supplied by Cockerell; he bought a gold coin for £50 as well as Rhodian marble vases and, on Prince Ludwig's particular recommendation, a skull; he also began excavating the theatre he had purchased on Melos. But, maintaining a stoical severity towards himself and driven by a sense of duty that, pushed to extremes, was almost a weakness, he attempted to accomplish too much; he succumbed at Ambelakia in the Vale of Tempe to a fever caught whilst digging out a tomb in September 1817. He was buried in the Theseion. He and Cockerell had planned to produce a text, illustrated by examples from their well-filled portfolios, which was to be the complete and final authority on Greek architecture and the grand result of their many years of travel; the loss of Haller's help disheartened Cockerell who, in addition, after his return to England in 1816, found himself overwhelmed with architectural commissions; it was not till 1859 that a truncated version was published by him alone.

Foster became a successful architect in his native Liverpool where the Monument of Lysicrates is recalled in his St George's Church. Brøndsted, Linckh and Stackelberg retreated to Italy to pursue their interest in antiquity.

They had all garnered a small harvest of antiquities apart from the Aegina and Bassae marbles. Cockerell presented his Parthenon piece and his fragment of Bassae capital to the British Museum, but when his bull of Pentelic marble was being landed at London, the sailors let it slip into the Thames and fishing it out cost so much that he declined to pay the freight charges; the bull remained in the London custom house till rescued for Mr Mills, owner of Hillingdon Court near West Drayton; it was later presented to the museum by Lord Hillingdon. Brøndsted and Linckh had unearthed a number of marble fragments on the island of Kea in 1811, including the torso of a woman, part of a small female statue, the feet of another, and a female head, probably a caryatid; all were transported direct to Malta by a friendly sea-captain but their subsequent fate is uncertain. The vases, coins, gems and curiosities they had all collected were dispersed with scarcely a trace after their deaths. It is through their publications that they best served the cause of antiquity.

8

MELOS

The natural harbour of the island of Melos provided a safe anchorage for the ancient Greeks, and on the hill above they built a city enclosed by massive walls and crowned by an acropolis. It was here that was found a statue of Venus that is today one of the glories of the Louvre.

The Aegean islands had been a profitable source of antiquities ever since the seventeenth century, when Sir Kenelm Digby appropriated a quantity of marbles on Delos for Charles I. They were on the routes of what trade there was in the Levant, and travellers found in their often prosperous little towns more amusement and better fare than on the mainland, for the administration was almost entirely in the hands of the Greeks, the Muslims contenting themselves with an annual visit to exact tribute (£1,000 a year in the case of Melos) and to render justice with a promptitude equalled only by its ignorance.

The most striking antiquity on Melos was the Hellenistic theatre, whose well-preserved remains were purchased in 1816 by Haller on behalf of the Crown Prince of Bavaria but remained unexcavated until 1836 owing to the architect's tragic death. Some inscribed marbles were also found, two of which were appropriated by an Englishman, Salt, better known for his collecting activities in Egypt; one was said to have formed part of a large inscription that a bigoted priest had obliged the inhabitants to break in pieces in order to discourage collecting Franks who might disturb his holy retreat.

Not long afterwards, the French consul at Smyrna, M. David, invited his agents in the archipelago to buy for him any antiquities they could discover. Such agents were employed throughout the Levant by most western countries, their duties rendering them personages of importance in proportion to the political influence of the nation whose colours they mounted upon the flagstaff at their residence; and though possessed of no legal authority, their influence in their respective islands was by no means inconsiderable. The French and English took the lead, although the former bore a manifest superiority in the eyes of the Greeks which might be unequivocally attributed to the embroidered coat and sword of office which they assumed, or so the English consul of Tinos must have thought, for he sported in 1823 nothing less than the uniform of an English general, somewhat the worse for wear, to be sure; a star upon his left breast, a cocked hat and tremendous plume, jackboots, spurs, and a huge sword.

The English agents were usually native to the country, but the French generally appointed their own nationals and one of the most active of these was Consul Brest of the island of Melos. He lived in the largest village, Kastro, which clung to the hilltop site below the ancient acropolis, its whitewashed houses linked by irregular stone steps, its streets overhanging each other. Here, on the 'Eagle's Nest' overlooking a large expanse of sea, sat the islanders, well supplied with English telescopes; whoever first spotted a ship had the right to offer himself as pilot, sailing out to meet vessels sometimes at a distance of fifteen miles.

The French naval squadron in the Levant was well known to them, being in the habit of using their harbour for re-provisioning, laundry, rest and recreation. The sloops *Estafette* and *Lionne* arrived there on 4 March 1820 and on 8 April were still in the harbour. This is the date by which it is certain that the Venus de Milo had been unearthed.

Where the remains of the ancient city of Melos extended down the hillside, the ground was covered with fragments of columns and pieces of statues of such a nature as to bespeak former magnificence; here and there were huge outcrops of walls of very solid construction. A Greek peasant, Yorgos, his son Antonio and his nephew were digging their patch of ground near by when they uncovered several blocks of dressed stone. As such blocks had a value as building material, they decided to dig deeper, finally clearing a kind of oblong niche in which they found a marble statue of a nude female figure in two halves, as well as two pillar steles and various other fragments of sculpture. These included a hand holding an apple: the apple of discord it would seem, for so began the contentions that have surrounded the Venus de Milo ever since; as Fauvel caustically put it, if she no longer holds the apple in her hand, it is doubtless because she has thrown it into the archaeological cockpit.

Brest was immediately informed of the discovery. He in turn notified the officers of the French ships then in the harbour and took them to view the statue. Opinions were divided as to her worth, so Brest decided to write to his superior in Smyrna giving him the differing appreciations. The captain of one of the ships did likewise, adding that the statue represented Venus holding the apple of discord. The peasant Yorgos was anxious to sell her, but Brest being unwilling to commit himself, it was agreed that she should be reserved for him pending a decision from Smyrna.

Now comes the first uncertainty: Voutier, who was an ensign on board the *Estafette*, then in the harbour, told a different story of the discovery in a brochure published some fifty-four years afterwards. According to this, he had undertaken some excavations below the citadel rock, and whilst he was watching his two diggers—sailors from his ship—a peasant working some twenty paces from them discovered a little chapel. Voutier approached: the peasant had unearthed what looked like the upper part of a damaged and armless statue and was going to rebury it, but for a few piastres agreed to take it out. Voutier maintained that he was the one to inform Brest and that he then returned to the site with his album and sketched the statue. The peasant had meanwhile found two pillar steles with inscriptions, and an arm.

Many years later also, Brest produced yet another version,

according to which he had had the Venus transferred to his house immediately after the discovery, only to have her stolen by competitors and placed on board a disused ship. This is presumably a fantasy, but it helped to confuse the issue.

We can at least be certain that the statue had been seen by several French officers by the time their ships left Melos on 11/12 April with the news of the discovery. They arrived at Smyrna on 26 April.

Meanwhile, on 16 April, the French corvette *Chevrette*, sailing from Toulon, anchored in the harbour of Melos.

Lieutenant Dumont d'Urville, accompanied by the second-in-command of the corvette, Lieutenant Matterer, paid a visit to Brest who took the two young men to see the statue. After viewing the niche where the lower half only still remained, they found the upper portion had been moved to a miserable little hut in the corner of the peasant's plot, where his mother spun while she watched over the treasure. Who would have thought, wrote Matterer, that the statue therein was later to be placed in the most beautiful museum in Europe? The two officers stood stupefied at the aspect of the superb figure that seemed about to speak to them. It appeared to be in the best of taste, but, conscious of their inadequate knowledge of the arts, they had no confidence in their opinion.

Dumont describes the statue as being about six feet high and representing a female figure, whose raised left hand held an apple; the right held up a drapery artfully disposed and falling negligently from the hips to the feet. Both arms, however, had been damaged and were detached from the torso. This was because, in the same way as the statue had been made in two parts joined by clamps, the left arm certainly, the right possibly, had been fashioned separately, designed to be maintained in position by tenons; the socket for that of the left arm can clearly be seen today. The hair, also separate when the statue was found, was easily replaced in position and was seen to be drawn back and held by a bandeau. The face was very beautiful and well preserved except for some damage to the nose. The one remaining foot was bare and half-covered by the hem of the drapery. The ears were pierced and must have held ear-rings.

All these attributes, says Dumont, seemed to match those of the Venus of the Judgement of Paris; but where, then, he wondered, were the other two contestants, Juno and Minerva, and the handsome shepherd boy? It is true that, at the same time, a sandalled foot and a third hand had been discovered; could these have belonged to the apparently missing protagonists? One thing is certain: detached and damaged as the different parts of the statue were, those who first saw her identified her as Venus holding the apple of discord.

Yorgos the peasant wanted to sell her there and then, but the two young Frenchmen could not accept: first, they had not sufficient cash between them; second, their ship was due to undertake a voyage in the Black Sea and their captain would not have countenanced the embarkation of a large, heavy statue; he was interested in hydrographic surveying, not antiquities; finally, the two friends still did not feel themselves able to judge of the value of the statue; as they both admitted later, they were hardly well inspired in refusing. However, once they had sailed from Melos, Dumont set to work, in the silence of his small cabin, to draw up an historical and descriptive note of the Venus.

BATTLE OF WORDS OR DEEDS

The *Chevrette* arrived at Constantinople on 28 April. The French ambassador, the Marquis de Rivière, had already been informed of the find and, on hearing Dumont's opinion, decided to buy. Fortunately, one of the embassy secretaries, the Comte de Marcellus, was about to leave on a duty tour of the eastern Mediterranean in the sloop *Estafette*, which had been at Melos when the statue was discovered; he was instructed to purchase. The *Estafette* sailed on 15 May and, after visits to Syros and Delos, arrived at Melos on 22 May. Marcellus was nearly too late.

Brest had also been instructed, by the consul at Smyrna, to buy the statue and had made every effort to conclude his bargain with

Yorgos at a price of £15 and a coat worth 9 shillings. But he had a rival: a monk who, accused of financial malpractice, hoped to regain the favour of the administrator of the islands, Nikolaki Morusi, by making him a present of the beautiful marble. Morusi, the dragoman of the Turkish High Admiral, came of a well-known Greek family resident in the Phanar district of Constantinople, a colony that provided much of the administrative personnel of the Ottoman Government. An Englishman witnessed his progress through the islands at this time: the young gentleman, aged twenty-five, wore a splendid dress and was surrounded by some eighty hungry Greeks, who behaved to him with the greatest obsequiousness and indemnified themselves by a corresponding insolence to the islanders.

A kind of auction had ensued for the Venus and the whole village had been drawn into the controversy. The monk could point to the advantages to be derived from gaining the favour of Morusi; Brest could stress the value of the French naval customers who visited the port, but the protection of his ambassador would not weigh as heavily as that of the reigning overlord. He fought hard; but as Marcellus's ship arrived, the statue, brought down from the hilltop village, was in the custody of the rival party. The crew of the *Estafette* saw a rowing-boat heavily laden proceeding towards a ship lying in the harbour. Somebody said laughingly: 'There goes our statue.' It was only too true: the Venus was being embarked on a ship ready to leave for Constantinople.*

Marcellus did not give up hope; led by some instinct, he tells us, he determined to overcome the obstacles confronting him and resolved, with the fiery impetuosity of a young heart eager to fight against what seemed impossible odds, to gain possession of the statue at any price. He told Lieutenant Robert, commander of the *Estafette*, that if the rival ship showed signs of hoisting sail, she should be stopped from leaving at all costs; luckily the north

---

* This ship may have been named *Galixidion* or merely have been based on the port of Galixidi; thus she may have been a Greek vessel trading under the Turkish flag or even the Austrian one; Brest later alleged that she was Russian.

wind came on to blow, the only one that closed the harbour. Then he entered into long and frustrating negotiations with the local elders; unwearyingly he argued that the statue would not be thought valuable in Constantinople in view of the well-known aversion of the Turks to representations of the human face and form in general and damaged statues of idols in particular; he urged that Morusi would never be able to get the statue restored to make good the damage caused by time, by the digging up and in transit. He attempted to board the rival ship to see the Venus, but the captain ran up his flag while his crew manned the bulwarks aiming their muskets at the French party. For his part, Marcellus was backed up by the respect always inspired by a ship of war and the strong arms of the fifty sailors of the *Estafette*. Finally, after two days of haggling, it was agreed that the Venus should be sold to the French at the cash price the monk had promised to pay; Marcellus added a third as much again, making some £30 in all. The Venus was forthwith removed to the *Estafette* and Marcellus could at last see and admire his prize, could contemplate the superhuman beauty, the gentle majesty, of that divine figure.

But Matterer, who had been amongst the first to see the statue, is said to have told a different tale some years later:* that of a pitched battle for possession of the statue. He was not an eyewitness, being in the Black Sea at the time; two members of the *Estafette*'s crew who were, far from corroborating him, stated that the statue had been handed over from the rival ship without a fight.

Matterer's story runs as follows. When Marcellus arrived at Melos, the Venus was lying on the shore awaiting embarkation on the rival ship and surrounded by a group of men. He realised that there might be a fight if he attempted to seize her, since the monk had a good many of the inhabitants on his side for religious reasons; he determined to risk it. He said to Lieutenant Robert: 'We had best arm ourselves with swords and pistols and take twenty ratings with us, also armed.' No sooner had they landed

* Cf J. Aicard, *Recherches sur l'histoire de la découverte de la Venus de Milo*, 1874.

than a tremendous argument started around the Venus, the Greeks seeming determined not to let the French have her. Suddenly Robert, nicknamed Robert-le-Diable, a man of action, shouted: '*A moi, mes matelots*: take up the Venus and hoist her on board our boat.' Battle commenced: swords and sticks flew, blows fell on the heads and backs of the monk and of the poor Greeks, who cried out in despair and called on God to rain thunderbolts on Marcellus, Robert and Brest, for the latter gentleman was lending a hand armed with a sword and a stout stick. An ear was cut off; blood flowed. But during the battle the French sailors managed to seize the statue from out of the mêlée, get it on board their boat and bear it off in triumph to the *Estafette*. 'If the statue had been changed to flesh and blood, how bitterly would she have wept to find herself dragged over the beach, jolted and rolled about by angry men,' commented Matterer. One is none the less reminded of the unfounded rumour of the destruction of the Corinthian capital from Bassae.

Yet another later and even more suspect version by Brest combined the two accounts: he stated that, assisted by an officer and twelve men from the *Estafette*, he had recovered the statue from the rival ship 'by main force'. He also produced a story of an English attempt to procure the Venus, made by two mysterious lords offering vast sums (£1,000) whom he proudly sent away empty-handed; but it is true that the *Estafette* passed an English and a Dutch ship off Melos, both from Malta, both, it was said, hoping to be first in the queue to purchase the Venus, both disappointed of the prize.

It is also true that the Venus sustained some damage. Traces of the ropes that had been knotted round her to facilitate transport showed clearly; but, far more serious, her shoulders and parts of her back and hips had received score-marks and on the shoulders the marble was so bruised that it flaked away, leaving wounds several inches wide. Marcellus blamed the monk for taking no precautions to protect the marbles when transporting them down to the beach; the flinty paths that wound down to the harbour were certainly steep and narrow, resembling nothing so much as a broken staircase, and he could be right. Matterer contended that the statue was damaged during the battle on the shore; this would perhaps explain why her first visitors all reached the same conclusion as to the probable position of her arms, whereas when she reached Paris, her accompanying fragments did not produce the same consensus of opinion. Were parts of those arms left shattered on the beach?

The possibility that there had been a battle for the statue was for many years kept discreetly quiet. Such a proceeding would have appeared far from dignified, and Marcellus would naturally prefer it to be thought that the arts of diplomacy rather than the muscular prowess of his sailors had saved her from the infidel. Was it a battle of words or deeds?

Morusi's fury at being deprived of the intended bribe was unbounded. He swore that he would rather have seen the Venus consigned to the bottom of the sea than handed over to the French; Brest and the other Frenchmen should have been stoned; he did not recognise the existence of all these consuls in the islands, and if the Melos agent dared to excavate or buy any more statues, the inhabitants of Kastro were authorised to kill him. He then officially banned everyone but the monk from dealing in antiquities, condemned the local officials to a fine of £150 and had them flogged in front of the assembly of Greek dignitaries of the islands.

The French ambassador was not prepared to allow Morusi to proffer with impunity such an insult to the French nation. He insisted to the Sublime Porte that the local officials be indemnified; this was promised but never carried out and the consul at Smyrna had to suffer their complaints till, five years later, the French Admiral de Rigny took a hand and notified Paris. Rivière immediately supplied the necessary funds which were paid over in return for a receipt signed and sealed by the municipality: the Venus had thus cost him less than £200.

Morusi's reaction constituted an unwelcome complication of the affair for Marcellus. They had been good friends; of the same age, they had fraternised when Marcellus was at Constantinople;

he could not understand the inconstancy of Morusi's friendship or forgive the diplomatic ructions that had resulted. But they never met again; Morusi was suspected by the Turks of complicity in the Greek revolt of 1821 and was executed at Constantinople.

We must now return to the fate of the Venus. On board the *Estafette* Marcellus had her carefully sewn into canvas sacks: the bust in one, the lower part in a second, and the detached hair-piece, a damaged part of a forearm and a half a hand holding an apple, and the accompanying steles, separately. The sacks were laid on mattresses to avoid further damage. And there they stayed for four months while Marcellus completed his tour to Rhodes, Cyprus, Alexandria, the Piraeus and back to Smyrna. The captive Venus was thus transported round the eastern Mediterranean, to be uncovered for admiring inspection wherever there were amateurs and to endure the unpredictable storms that could put navigators into such 'plaguey frights'. Marcellus took the greatest pleasure in showing her to Fauvel at the Piraeus. Late one September evening they proceeded on board the *Estafette*. Marcellus undid the sacks, propped the Venus up and put her hair in place. Fauvel wanted to see her first by moonlight only; then torches were brought. He viewed her from every angle, explaining her beauty, commenting on the fine workmanship. Finally he said: 'I came to Greece young like you along with other passionately devoted antiquarians; we grew old in our investigations. But never did any of us meet on our way such a piece of good fortune as you in obtaining this Venus.'

At Smyrna, the sacks were transferred aboard the *Lionne* and left for France with the ambassador, destined as a personal gift of homage to the king and for the enrichment of the Louvre. By March 1821, the Venus had arrived in Paris, and a commemorative medal was struck. She excited the greatest admiration, even being placed equal to the less well-preserved Parthenon marbles that the British Museum had by now acquired. But the savants were soon asking for an exact account of her discovery so that they could restore and date her. Forbin, the Keeper of Antiquities at the Louvre, had a report ready by the end of 1822; so many persons had claimed the honour of the discovery* that, to dissipate all doubts, he had consulted that Nestor of oriental antiquaries, Fauvel. This gentleman, after remarking that there were few discoveries that had not provoked lively disputes between their discoverers, saw no reason to doubt the account of Marcellus and congratulated Rivière on being enabled to present the king with a gift unmatched by all the oriental bits and pieces with which every Gaulish, German or Pict ambassador loaded his baggage on his recall.

THE APPLE OF DISCORD

Another battle now commenced: the controversy over the original pose of the Venus. The lack of reliable recording of the discovery was partly to blame, a lack that was characteristic of the methods of retrieval of the time. Every collection in Europe contained remains of antiquity that had become inexplicable because of ignorance of their origin. The British Museum catalogue recorded some curious provenances: 'found in a store at Portsmouth', 'perhaps brought from Cyzikus by H.M.S. *Blonde* in 1830', equalled only by an origin recorded in the catalogue of the Guildhall Museum: 'Tottenham Court Road'. Elgin's collection contained over twenty fragments whose find-places were unknown. No attempt was, of course, made to record the context in which antiquities were found. It seems extraordinary today that scholars failed to realise that many problems of dating and attribution could have been solved if the artefacts found with the desirable objects, however humble and broken, had been noted as evidence instead of being discarded as rubbish. If only one of the many first sighters of the Venus had made a proper record of how, where and with what she had been unearthed!

Marcellus only listed the fragments he got on board his ship. Two of these were crucial for determining her original attitude: half of a hand holding an apple and a piece of a forearm; but did these really match the torso in scale, material, technique and

* For a bibliography, cf S. Reinach, *Revue Archaeologique,* 1906, pp 199ff.

traces of weathering? Several experts denied it. The situation was further confused when the ambassador later called at Melos and brought away two more fragmentary arms. The field was thus open for every kind of theory as to the pose given to her by her creator: holding a shield or a mirror, forming part of a pair with Paris or Mars, perhaps not Venus at all, but the nymph Melos, the personification of the island, or a victory blowing a trumpet. The result is that her arms have never been restored: fortunately, in view of the incongruous additions accorded to other statues both before and after.

More controversy was to come: was the Venus a work of Praxiteles, as everyone wanted to believe? Or was she of much later date, perhaps the work of the sculptor from Antioch on the Meander, a city founded only in 260 BC, whose name was inscribed on part of the plinth that disappeared shortly after its arrival at the Louvre with her? Accused of voluntarily mislaying what might be evidence that she must date from after 260 BC, the authorities even dug up the floor of the Louvre cellars in a vain search for it. Another inscribed marble is also missing: that from over the niche, though we have the copy of the lettering, made in 1821. Yet a third inscription was missing until this century: the base of the second stele, discovered supporting a different one in the Louvre galleries. Certainly, in those early museum days, marbles were apt to lie about anyhow; certainly, any piece conveniently to hand ran the risk of being re-utilised for a restoration; but to mislay three out of three is unusual.

The general opinion now is that the Venus is a work of the latter half of the second or of the first century BC, which is no reason for esteeming her at less than her engaging worth.

A final discord was provided by the King of Bavaria, who claimed that the Venus had been found in the theatre purchased for him by Haller and that she therefore belonged to him. However, he had eventually to recognise that her niche had been about 500 paces from his site and he withdrew from the arena.

The harbour had returned to harmony by the time Emerson and his friends visited it in 1825.

We found our sailors collected round an itinerant musician, who accompanied himself on a kind of guitar, whilst the seamen danced their Romaika to his monotonous chant. Their motions were rapid, violent and intricate: they swung round, stooped towards the earth, and sprung aloft till they touched the soles of their feet with their fingers and then, joining hands, they again threaded the mazes of the dance, all the time wearing as much solemnity in their countenances as if engaged in some mysterious ceremony of their church. Our boat was detained whilst the musician, who seemed to be a well-known and popular performer, was solicited to sing the favourite ballad of each of the audience who could advance him a coin. Of the sweetness of them, any translation can give but a faint idea. The Greeks were so enchanted by his performance that even the approach of night could not induce them to break up. With some difficulty we prevailed on two of them to row us on board, and as we glided slowly over the unrippled water we could still hear the alternate plaudits of the sailors and the clear tones of the minstrel as he sang by the shores of the moonlit bay.

9

CRY HAVOC

DAMAGE AND DESTRUCTION

The dogs of war were unleashed in 1821 when the Greeks rose
against their Turkish oppressors; for the next seven years the
imperatives were: kill, burn and destroy. By 1825, Athens presented a wretched picture of desolation, her narrow streets
blocked by ruined houses; travellers had been known to complain
that the frivolity and gossip of the modern town detracted from
the serious impression that should be made by the ancient ruins;
now there was only desolation around the temples and monuments, and even they seemed to be hurrying to decay with a
quicker pace than ordinary; indeed, the Turks declared an intention of destroying them totally, since their presence appeared to
help keep alive the spirit of the Greeks besides exciting a feeling of
sympathy for the insurgents in the breasts of Europeans.

During the first siege of the Acropolis, the embattled Turks,
short of bullets, demolished the south-west end of the Parthenon
cella to get at the lead filling the spaces round the iron clamps;
they also broke up the drums of the fallen columns to make
cannon-balls; miraculously, no standing column was overthrown
in the bombardments, though several were damaged by shot. The
Erechtheion suffered severely in 1827, when the Greeks had
gained possession of the citadel: Turkish shot displaced the north-
west angle columns of the porch and the marble roof gave way,
crushing in its fall a number of Athenian ladies residing within it

for safety. One of the remaining caryatids was also shot away, bringing down with it part of the architrave and roof.*

The Monument of Lysicrates had a narrow escape. The visitor Alcock, fearing that it would fall a prey to Turkish vengeance, obtained permission from their commander to remove it in return for European articles of much more use to him; but Alcock soon realised that it would be difficult to remove a monument weighing eight tons and might deserve the reproach of despoiling Greece of that which might still be an object of pride to her in her dawn of freedom; he desisted. Next, the Turks set fire to the surrounding monastery and the heat of the conflagration caused some of the frieze to crack and fall; but help was forthcoming in the combined efforts of Gropius and the French consulate: the ruins of the convent were demolished and the Monument temporarily shored up. The Theseion had been struck by lightning on 13 May 1821, some six feet of the cornice being carried away and a drum of the angle column split so that the sky could be seen through the opening; some pious hand surrounded it with an iron band to hold it together. The interior was disgracefully degraded, for the Turks turned it into a stable and the floor was soon deep in dung; they also opened the Christian graves in search of treasure, scattering the contents about. This explains the loss of many of the gravestones, though some French visitors reinterred the most recently buried remains.

In the Morea, the damage incidental to war was typified at Megalopolis, where the remaining marble was removed from the theatre to fortify Karitena. Elsewhere, westerners continued to help themselves to the remains. At Sunion, the Austrian admiral Paulucci sequestered several column drums, depositing them at the Arsenal of Venice; he then inflicted dreadful vandalism in the shape of an inscription in black paint of the name of his vessel along the entire length of the temple frieze: '*Bellona Austriaca*,

---

* Though travellers helped themselves to pieces, this caryatid was restored in 1837; Lusieri's caryatid, the second from the left in front, has been replaced by an artificial stone cast; the rear one to the right that disappeared 100 years previously has been replaced by a modern reproduction.

1824' in letters that could be seen far at sea; an English midshipman commented in equally conspicuous characters: 'Buy Warren's Blacking'. Another Austrian—the envoy to Constantinople—obtained a decorative panel from Megara while Lord Strangford, the English ambassador, acquired marble fragments from Athens and his famous Archaic Apollo from one of the islands, probably Anaphe, where Fauvel saw a 'mountain of bad statues' newly unearthed about this time. The islands, indeed, suffered dreadfully from depredators, being so frequently visited by the crews of western squadrons; even the Americans took a hand on Melos where they excavated what was apparently a small odeon, finding four inscribed seats cut into a half-circle in a rock. A Dutch-protected merchant bought the land from which the Venus of Melos had been taken and found another niche with a damaged statue; it finished up in Berlin. A famous head that may be of Asclepios and a votive relief were also dug out in 1828; they were bought by the Duc de Blacas and are now in the British Museum. The island's tombs were systematically plundered, as were those of Aegina, where the inhabitants opened hundreds of graves to sell the contents to naval officers and diplomatic envoys alike when it was the seat of the Greek Government around 1829.

Fauvel at first remained at Athens: he was no Philhellene, regarding the Turks as the rightful lords of Greece; when a stray Turkish cannon-ball went through his roof, he was not unduly disturbed, but when their Acropolis garrison capitulated, he gathered up his archives and portable antiquities and took refuge at Smyrna under the kindly wing of the French consul, with a pension of £150, till his death in 1838. His museum was packed into fifty-four cases, but it was impossible to keep it together under war conditions: the Greeks refused him permission to export and his house was first turned into a refuge for the ransomed ladies of the Turkish harems and then destroyed; all trace of it soon disappeared except for a few fragmentary marbles, sad reminders of the former home of the famous collector.

Gropius remained, taking over Fauvel's role of cicerone and antiquarian. He was in a difficult position during the war, for

Austria, whose vice-consul he now was, was hostile to Greek aspirations, whereas the visitors were mostly Philhellenes. He partially succeeded in contenting both sides, for one traveller commented that, had he not been the agent of Austria, he would have been as great an enthusiast for Greek regeneration as he was for the preservation of her ancient remains; another, however, accused him of abusing General Church's friendship to convey military information to the Turks. All was forgotten, however, when, after the war, the new King Otho was presenting colours to the Greek regiments at Navplion; two pavilions occupied the centre of the ground: in one was the nascent government of Greece; the other shaded Madame Gropius, the Corps Diplomatique and Admiral Sir Pulteney Malcolm.

OLYMPIA AND THE FRENCH
EXPÉDITION DE MORÉE

Ever since the days of Winckelmann, antiquaries had dreamed of excavating Olympia. Little did they know that the site was almost naked, the only visible ruins in the sacred precinct of Zeus being those of the cella of a large temple, its stones all injured and manifesting the labour of persons who had endeavoured to remove the metal clamps that joined them.

Fauvel was there in 1797. Some peasants, seeking building materials, had dug out pieces of fluted columns more than six feet in diameter that had obviously belonged to the temple of Zeus, and he was able to trace the course of the cella walls; he also marked the position of the Olympic stadium but found that the contiguous hippodrome had been completely washed away by the river Alpheios in flood. None the less, he thought the site not wanting in portable (and profitable) objects of curiosity; to obtain these, it was best to await the autumn when the soil was moistened by rains; the traveller would then find at every step ancient bucklers, fragments of bas-reliefs and trophies of bronze; he himself purchased a helmet. Aberdeen was there in 1803 armed with firmans and presents but found the temple, he thought, well explored and left it alone; Smirke, Gell, Dodwell, Leake and Stackelberg all visited and measured; J. S. Stanhope and Allason surveyed the whole site thoroughly in 1814. Lusieri got as far as inducing the Pasha of the Morea to authorise diggings in return for £300 and a gold watch, but Elgin's flow of funds had dried up and nothing came of it.

By 1828, the War of Independence had been dragging on for seven years and the utter exhaustion of Greece prevented her from making any further effort to expel the Turko-Egyptian army from the Morea despite the naval victory of Navarino: the direct agency of the West was required. The French undertook to send a force to dislodge Ibrahim Pasha and his troops and on 30 August an army of 14,000 men landed on the Gulf of Coron to win the honour of delivering the Morea. But the work of the scientific commission that had accompanied Napoleon to the Nile and produced the *Description de l'Egypte* had not been forgotten; it was decided that a similar commission should be attached to this Greek force.

The first object of the archaeological section was to examine the ruins of Olympia. The head of this section, not a well-inspired choice, was J. J. Dubois, a minor employee of the Louvre and compiler of descriptive sale catalogues, entirely without the erudition or dignity necessary for the post, thought the scholar Lenormant who, though attached to the section, did not participate in its work. With the artists Duval and Trézel, Dubois proceeded early in May 1829 to Olympia; finding himself confronted by an indiscriminate and buried wreck, he began digging at the jetsam of the temple. The artistic section arrived a week later. Led by the seasoned architect Blouet, it comprised Ravoisié and Poirot, also architects, and the writer de Gournay. Blouet's workmen joined those of the archaeologists, but after four days Dubois put his men to excavate at the front of the temple while *les Blouet* directed theirs to the rear; dissensions between the teams presumably motivated this division of labour.

The finds were few: only the remains of some of the sculptured marble metopes that had ornamented both front and rear vestibules of the temple and had depicted the twelve labours of Hercules. Dubois had chosen the wrong end of the temple: he found only fragments of three metopes. Blouet, though he missed two well-preserved ones now in Olympia's museum, unearthed a

large portion of the combat with the bull of Crete and parts of
two others; then his men turned up a fragment they could not at
first fit into the description of the metopes given by Pausanias: a
figure of a girl sitting on a rock; she came perfect from the earth,
but some workmen, profiting from a moment when the Franks
were absent, broke her nose with a stone in an access of fanaticism; luckily, the accident could be easily repaired, for one of the
artists had already drawn the face. It was soon realised, however,
that the girl was Athene and had formed part of the metope
depicting Hercules' victory over the man-eating Stymphalian
birds. Only the leader of the scientific section, Colonel Bory de
St Vincent, could not credit this: to him, the charming figure
looked more like a shepherdess dreaming of her lover than the
proud divinity.

Dubois uncovered a large area in front of the temple; Blouet
cut trenches across the ground at the rear; but nothing more
could be found. This poor plunder dismayed those who had
hoped to unearth the famous pedimental sculptures—they were
discovered by the 1876 German excavations and are now in the
museum at Olympia. It had, of course been beyond their wildest
dreams to bring to light any remains of Phidias' gold and ivory
statue of Zeus, one of the seven wonders of the ancient world.

After six weeks the artists moved on to search for the faint
traces of former splendour in the ancient remains of the Morea.
The archaeological section, left behind, sank into complete
failure: Dubois became ill and, with Duval, retreated from Greece,
abandoning the heavier marbles at Olympia, taking only some
precious fragments as far as Navarino. But how was even this
scanty fruit to be got back to France? Peremptory removal, in the
philhellenic temper of the time, was out of the question; finally,
General Schneider, commander of the French forces, sought the
permission of the Greek Senate, which acquiesced. An artillery
company was despatched to Olympia; most of the finds were
loaded on to their wagons, but they experienced the greatest
difficulty in piercing a route to the coast; spurs of mountainside
had to be hacked away and ramps built over ravines and river

beds. The antiquities were then collected at Navarino where *les Blouet* supervised their despatch to France in October 1829. Thanks to the assistance of both army and navy, the sculptures had cost only the wages of the local workmen—perhaps £50.

The Louvre was later accused of having lost some fragments, but in the absence of certainty as to what was brought back—some of the marbles sketched by the artists were apparently left behind—it is impossible to be sure. Some additional items were secured: a bas-relief from Messene sent to France in 1828, and a female torso removed from the walls of the citadel at Patras by General Schneider. Blouet personally acquired some fragments, presented to the Louvre in 1863, and Dubois appropriated a helmet.

The expedition's report on the fine arts, published from 1831 onwards, had to be prepared solely by *les Blouet*, for Dubois had dropped out. Its three sumptuous volumes contained beautiful drawings and measurements of architecture, sculpture and inscriptions in the Morea, the islands and Attica, but it was going too far to maintain, as did the fiery Bory, that they had discovered the temple of Zeus at Olympia or even, as Blouet more modestly claimed, that its dedication had been only conjecture prior to their excavations: earlier travellers like Gell had identified it with certainty. Blouet correctly foresaw that the material booty would cause disappointment: the finds were not only few in quantity, but were not considered as of high quality, and the fact that much of the finishing had originally been effected by colouring was disconcerting. In addition, in a fashion characteristic of the infancy of archaeology, the artists were censured for not having dug out the ancient cities they had only briefly visited, as if it had been feasible for a handful of men to probe in a few days enormous sites that were later to demand years of scientific excavation. One critic had the grace to admit that the island of Delos might perhaps have been too much for them to tackle.

EPILOGUE

Antiquity-hunting in Greece between 1800 and 1830 had been profitable. Though Elgin would never have recovered his costs even if he had sold abroad, Fauvel made a tidy income out of his trading, the Aegina marbles produced a sizeable return for their discoverers and the Bassae society did even better; presentation of the Eleusis Ceres and the Venus de Milo brought only honour to Clarke and Cripps and to the Marquis de Rivière, but their outlay had been small; the state-aided removals from Olympia were most economical. Thereafter, however, profitability started to disappear: private enterprise could no longer bear the mounting costs of excavation and transport; the accessible sites had been denuded and material difficulties farther afield were daunting. Furthermore, the Greeks, in their new-found independence, were increasingly reluctant to allow their cultural assets to be plundered.

This was not an entirely new development. Though Greek masons were great destroyers of the remains of antiquity, more lettered persons, who had some respect for the ancient fame of the nation, had been in the habit of preserving inscribed or sculptured stones by depositing them in churches or private houses. In 1813, the Philomousoi, a society of Greek and Frank lovers of letters and arts, was founded in Athens, the Hon F. North becoming its first president. Cockerell, Foster, Haller and their friends were all members, as were the three Makri sisters, and every well-informed stranger who visited the town was invited to join; the society's aims were mainly educational, but it was also intended to set up a museum with the antiquities abandoned by travellers, though nothing came of this plan. Caroline, Princess of Wales, became a patroness of the flourishing school in 1816 and the library rapidly increased. Fauvel did not join, and his comments must have been acid if they are reflected by Pouqueville, who considered that the society was neither learned nor educational and that the professors taught only the virtues of rebellion against the kind of peace that was all a subjugated Greece could hope for. He found one of the pupils useful, however, in copying inscriptions for him.

The Philomousoi tried to promote the protection of ancient monuments during the war and in 1822 were suggesting to the government the demolition of shops built against the Corinthian colonnade of Hadrian's library which presented a fire risk. In 1824, spurred by Colonel Stanhope, they were reorganising themselves with wider aims, and the busy colonel himself induced the Greek chieftain Odysseus, then Governor of Athens, to use the mosque in the Parthenon as a depot for antiquities transported by Turkish prisoners; not surprisingly, this came to nothing, but a museum was established on the island of Aegina in 1829. Space at the newly built orphanage was reserved and a keeper appointed; the catalogue mentions a quantity of vases, inscriptions, statues and bas-reliefs, the majority of which had come from the islands. As soon as conditions became more settled, the antiquities were removed to Athens, where buildings such as the Theseion served as provisional depots, soon filled to overflowing. Even Sparta had its little museum.

One more danger to the Acropolis was averted. Ludwig, now King of Bavaria, whose son Otho had become the first King of Greece, ardently desired to see Athens restored to all her ancient glory. He requested the renowned architect Schinkel to prepare a plan for the restoration of the Acropolis buildings and the construction of a royal residence at the vacant eastern end. The scheme fortunately never got beyond the drawing-board.

In May 1834 the first law to prevent the random excavation and unrestricted export of Greece's heritage was promulgated. By the end of that year, the newly formed Greek Archaeological Service had started work on the Acropolis; two years later, the temple of Athene Nike had been rebuilt, the site had been cleared of houses and debris, and the machinery and scaffolding needed for the raising of the columns of the Parthenon had been prepared.

GLOSSARY

ACROTERIA upright ornaments set above the three angles of a
temple pediment

ANTAE terminals of projecting side walls of a temple porch,
usually pilasters

ARCHAIC artistic productions of approximately the seventh and
sixth centuries BC, sculpture usually characterised by fixed
'Archaic smile'

ARCHITRAVE or EPISTYLE horizontal beams laid on column
capitals

CAVEA semi-circular auditorium of a theatre comprising rising
tiers of seats

CELLA the inner chamber of a temple, usually surrounded by a
colonnade

COFFERED CEILING panels, recessed and usually decorated,
between ceiling beams

CORINTHIAN capitals carved with acanthus-leaf sprays, see
p 138, single capital on the left

CORNICE horizontal: line of stone blocks laid above frieze;
sloping or raking: edging to the roof bounding the pediment

DIMINUTION tapering of column shaft from bottom up

DORIC columns without bases, plain cushion capitals, see p 138,
surrounding columns

DRUMS separately hewn sections from which column shaft built
up

Glossary

ENTABLATURE   architectural elements above the columns and capitals

EPISTYLE   see ARCHITRAVE

FRIEZE   decorative band above architrave. Doric: alternate blocks, triglyphs and metopes; Ionic: often continuous sculptured band

HELLENISTIC   pertaining to approximately the last three centuries BC, sculpture becoming more realistic, individual, emotive and even sensational

IONIC   columns on moulded bases; capitals comprise cushion usually carved with egg and tongue decoration on which rests volute member like a bolster with ends rolled inwards (rams' horns); see p 138, single capital on the right

METOPE   in Doric frieze, almost square blocks, often sculptured, alternating with triglyphs

NAOS   usually the principal inner chamber of a temple; see CELLA

PEDIMENT   triangular area bounded by horizontal and raking cornices above entablature of temple, often containing sculpture

PRONAOS   vestibule or porch in front of the naos of a temple

STELE   upright slab, usually inscribed or sculptured

STOA   a row of columns carrying an entablature, attached to a building as a porch or standing independently

STYLOBATE   platform on which a temple stands

TRIGLYPH   in Doric frieze, blocks decorated with vertical bands and grooves, alternating with metopes

TYMPANUM   vertical back wall of the pediment of a temple

BIOGRAPHICAL AND
BIBLIOGRAPHICAL INDEX

Aberdeen, 4th Earl of, Hamilton Gordon (1784–1860) Travelled in France, Italy and Greece 1802–3, connected with Gropius; founded Athenian Society and elected President of Society of Antiquaries 1812; lost interest in antiquities in favour of diplomacy and politics, Prime Minister 1852–5. 'Historical View of the Rise and Progress of Architecture amongst the Greeks', prefaced to Wilkins's translation of Vitruvius, 1812, published separately as *Inquiry into the Principles of Beauty in Grecian Architecture*, 1822; MS diary of Greek tour in Dept of Antiquities, BM. Acquired votive reliefs from Athens Pnyx, passed to BM with Elgin's by chance; Amyclean marbles presented to BM with other specimens 1861; 'Aberdeen' head of Hermes(?) and bronze helmet bought by BM; a sepulchral votive relief at Fitzwilliam, Cambridge; the remainder of his acquisitions are lost.

Aglio, Agostino (1777–1857) Accompanied Wilkins from Rome to Greece 1802, then to England, assisting in production of Wilkins's *Magna Graecia*; became well-known interior decorator.

Alcock, Thomas (1801–66) Served in army, then MP. *Travels in Russia, Persia, Turkey and Greece in 1828–9*, 1831.

Allason, Thomas (1790–1852) Visited Greece with J. S. Stanhope 1814; became well-known architect, designing many villas, mansions and public buildings. *Pictures and Views of the Antiquities of Pola*, 1819; *Quarterly*, 1821, pp 204ff.

Barry, Sir Charles, RA (1795–1860) On small inheritance, set out 1817 for France and Italy, Greece and Turkey with Eastlake etc; engaged by D. Baillie as travelling artist till 1820; became famous architect, Houses of Parliament, etc. Drawings at RIBA.

Bartholdy, Jakob Ludwig (1779–1825) Prussian diplomat and connoisseur, travelled 1803–4 in France, Italy and Levant, partly with Aberdeen and Gropius; 1815, Prussian consul-general for Italy. *Voyage en Grèce*, translation 1807.

Bedford, Francis (1784–1858) Member of 1811 Dilettanti expedition; exhibited RA 1814–32 and designed churches in London. Travel sketchbooks and drawings at RIBA.

Blouet, Abel (1795–1853) Grand Prix de Rome in architecture, studied in Italy 1821–6; 1827, Government civil architect; 1829, headed artistic section of Expédition de Morée; 1832, replaced Huyot for completion of Arc de Triomphe; 1846–52, Professor of Architecture, Académie des Beaux-Arts. Fine arts volumes of publication of Expédition; various building treatises. Acquisitions: see Chapter 10, p 177.

Bory de St Vincent, Colonel J. B. G. M. (1778–1846) Under Napoleon combined military career with pursuit of natural science; headed scientific section of Expédition de Morée 1829; also mission to Algeria 1840. Physical science volumes of publication of Expédition; *Relation du voyage de la commission scientifique de Morée*, 2 vols, 1836–8; *Exploration de l'Algérie*, 1846, etc.

Bosset, Colonel Charles Philip de (1773–1845) Swiss; Governor of Cephalonia, 1810–14, then inspector of Ionian militia; retired 1818. *Essai sur les médailles de Cephalonie et de l'Ithaque*, 1815; *Parga and the Ionian Islands*, 1821. Acquired votive reliefs and coins bought by BM.

Brøndsted, Peter Oluf (1780–1842) Danish traveller and antiquarian; 1809, visited Italy, 1810–13, Greece and Levant with

Koes, Haller, etc participating in excavation of Bassae marbles; 1819, in Rome; 1821, revisited Greece, alternating in subsequent years between Denmark, England and France. *Voyages dans la Grèce*, two parts only published 1826–30; *Uber den Aufsatz im Hermes*, pamphlet refuting allegation in *Hermes* Vol 33 that he had plagiarised Villoisin's MSS, Paris and Stuttgart, 1830; various other antiquarian publications. Acquisitions: see Chapter 7.

Burgon, Thomas (1787–1858) Levant merchant, excavated at Athens and Melos 1809–13. *Enquiry into the Motives of the Ancients in their choice of Representation on coins*, 1838. Acquired bronzes, coins and vases, eg Burgon amphora, now in BM bought in 1842.

Byron, George Gordon, 6th Baron (1788–1824) Travelled in Greece and Levant, partly with Hobhouse 1809–11; 1816, left England to reside in Italy; 1823, to Greece to support cause of independence, died at Missalonghi. We cite only *English Bards and Scotch Reviewers*, 1809 (refs to Elgin and Aberdeen); *Childe Harold*, cantos I and II, 1812; *Curse of Minerva*, printed but not published, 1812; *Letters and Journals*, ed L. A. Marchand, 1973.

Casenove, Henry (1788–1879) Son of London merchant, detained by Napoleon, escaped via Greece, at Athens 1811 with brother. *A Narrative in Two Parts*, written in 1812, printed anonymously by J. Compton, 1813.

Chateaubriand, Vicomte François-René de (1768–1848) Émigré of 1792, travelled in Greece, Levant, Africa and Spain 1806; Minister of Foreign Affairs under Restoration. Of his famous writings we cite only *Itinéraire de Paris à Jérusalem*, 1811. Acquired souvenir fragments from Athens, Sparta, Mycenae, etc.

Choiseul-Gouffier, Comte M. G. F. A. de (1752–1817) Toured Levant 1776 with Foucherot, Hilair and Kauffer, visiting Greek islands; appointed ambassador to Constantinople 1785, sent Fauvel to Athens as artistic representative; fled to Russia 1792, returned to France 1802 making his peace with Napoleon; regained most of his sequestered antiquities and built museum-house off Champs-Elysées to exhibit them. *Voyage pittoresque de la Grèce*, Vols I 1782, II 1809, III 1818. Acquired antiquities in Constantinople, Smyrna, etc as well as Fauvel's despatches from Athens; cf catalogue of sale by J. J. Dubois, 1818.

Clarke, Reverend Edward Daniel, LlD (1769–1822) Tutor to Cripps 1799–1802, touring northern Europe and Levant; ordained 1805, held two livings and lectureship in mineralogy at Cambridge. *Travels in Various Countries of Europe, Asia and Africa*, 8 vols, 1810–23; *Testimonies of Different Authors Respecting the Colossal Statue of Ceres . . .*, 1802; *Greek Marbles Brought from the Shores of the Euxine . . .*, 1809; W. Otter, *Life and Remains of E. D. Clarke*, 1824. Acquisitions: see Chapter 4; also MS from Patmos, sold to Bodleian for £1,000 and coins sold to R. P. Knight for £100.

Cockerell, Charles Robert (1788–1863) Son of architect S. P. Cockerell; assistant to Smirke in rebuilding Covent Garden Theatre; 1810–17, toured Turkey, Greece, Asia Minor, Sicily, Italy and France; a much-appreciated architect, built at Oxford, Cambridge, Bristol, Liverpool and London; 1840–56, Professor of Architecture at RA. *Quarterly*, 1819, pp 327ff; contribution on Sicily to 1830 volume of Dilettanti *Antiquities of Athens*; *Temples at Aegina and Bassae . . .*, 1860; MSS at Dept of Antiquities, BM. *Travels in Southern Europe and the Levant*, ed by S. P. Cockerell, 1903. Acquisitions: see Chapters 6 and 7.

Cousinéry, E. M. (1747–1835) From 1773, consular official at Smyrna, Rosetta and Salonika; 1793, lost post in revolutionary era and resided at Smyrna till 1803, when returned to France. Opuscules on numismatic subjects and *Voyage dans la Macédonie*, 1831. Assembled at least four collections of antique coins, see Chapter 4, p 75.

Craven, Hon Keppel (1779–1851) Connoisseur and friend of Gell, whom he accompanied at own expense on 1811 Dilettanti expedition to Greece and Levant; 1814, briefly chamberlain to Princess Caroline, resided thereafter in Italy.

Cripps, John Martin (*d* 1853) Travelled as pupil of Clarke to northern Europe and Levant 1799–1801, bringing back large collection of antiquities, curiosities, etc, see Chapter 4; settled on estate at Stantons, Sussex, becoming practical horticulturalist.

Dilettanti, *see* Society of Dilettanti.

Dodwell, Edward A. (1767–1832) Of independent means; prisoner of war of French, travelled in Levant on parole in 1801 and 1805–6; made 400 drawings and his artist, Pomardi, 600; resided later in Italy; connoisseur and antiquary. *A Classical and Topographical Tour through Greece . . .*, 1819; *Views of Greece*, 1821; *Views and descriptions of Cyclopean Remains in Greece and Italy*, 1834. Acquisitions: his 'museum' at Rome included, from Greece, bronzes, terracottas and vases, eg pyxis found near Corinth in 1805; marbles included an arm with a hand, a fragment of a horse's leg from the Parthenon, two heads and a female statuette from Athens and decorative fragments from the Parthenon, Erechtheion, Eleusis and Mycenae; the fate is unknown of other antiquities unearthed by him at the Piraeus and Delphi; the 'museum' was sold after his death in 1832 to King Ludwig of Bavaria; cf *Musée Dodwell*, published by Direction de l'Institut de Correspondence archaeologique, Rome, 1837.

Donaldson, Thomas Leverton (1795–1885) Travelled in Italy, Greece and Levant with W. Jenkins 1819–22; built *inter alia* Holy Trinity, South Kensington; 1841, Professor of Architecture, University College; 1863, President RIBA. *Selection of Ornamental Sculptures in the Louvre*, 1828; contributions to 1830 volume of Dilettanti, *Antiquities of Athens* (Bassae, Messene and Mycenae); *Collection of Examples of Doorways* (including Erechtheion), 1833; sketchbook at RIBA.

Douglas, Hon Frederick Sylvester, MP (1791–1819) Travelled Greece and Levant, partly with North, 1811–12; member of Select Committee on Elgin marbles. *Essay on Certain Points of Resemblance between the Ancient and Modern Greeks*, 1813.

Dubois, J. J. (*d* 1846) Travelled in Levant 1815; 1817, delineator of Egyptian Antiquities, Louvre; headed archaeological section of Expédition de Morée, 1829; then under-keeper, Dept of Antiquities, Louvre. *Choix de pierres gravées antiques recueillies pendant un voyage fait au Levant* . . ., 1817; catalogues of numerous collections, 1818 onwards. Acquisitions: see Chapter 10.

Dumont d'Urville, Amiral Jules-Sébastien-César (1790–1842) Joined French Navy 1810, studying natural history and science; 1819, member of hydrographic mission to Black Sea, participated in purchase of Venus de Milo; became famous explorer. We cite only *Relation de la campagne hydrographique de la galère la Chevrette dans le Levant et la Mer Noire*, in *Annales Maritimes*, 1812, p 149.

Dupré, Louis (1789–1837) Court painter 1811 to King of Westphalia who sent him to Italy to study; 1819, travelled Greece and Levant with Hyett, Hay and Vivian as their painter; settled in Paris 1831, mainly watercolourist, much of his work lithographed. *Voyage à Athènes et à Constantinople*, 1825.

Duval, Amaury (*b* 1808) Member of archaeological section of Expédition de Morée 1829; became well-known portraitist and muralist.

Eastlake, Sir Charles Lock, RA (1793–1865) Studied to become historical painter; 1816, left for Italy, visiting Greece 1818 with Barry, Kinnard and Johnson; 1830, returned to England, becoming famous artist, President of RA, Keeper, later Director, of National Gallery. *Contributions to the Literature of the Fine Arts*, 2nd series, with a memoir by his widow, 1870; sketches at RIBA.

Elgin, Thomas Bruce, 7th Earl of (1766–1841)   After military and diplomatic career, appointed ambassador at Constantinople 1798; used opportunity to arrange study of remains of Greek art in Ottoman Empire, with artists engaged in Sicily and Italy; 1803–6, detained by Napoleon in France; after difficulties in shipping and housing antiquities acquired by his mission, a Select Committee of House of Commons in 1816 established his right of ownership and propriety in removing them, recommending purchase for the nation for £35,000; subsequently took little part in public affairs. Cf W. St Clair, *Lord Elgin and the Marbles*, 1967; A. H. Smith, *Journal of Hellenic Studies*, 1916, pp 163ff; for detail of acquisitions cf *Catalogue of Sculptures at the BM*, 1892; Elgin retained some marbles, vases etc at his house, Broomhall.

Fauvel, Louis François Sebastien (1753–1838)   Travelled Italy and Greece with Foucherot for Choiseul-Gouffier 1780–2; 1785, returned to Levant in Choiseul's artistic suite; 1786, sent to Athens as artistic representative; 1787, in Constantinople, 1788, visited archipelago, 1789, fled the plague to Egypt, returning Athens with Choiseul's son; 1792, in Constantinople, left for Salonika with Cousinéry; 1793, returned Athens, where imprisoned 1799 after French invasion of Egypt; transferred to Constantinople, then repatriated 1801; 1803, returned to Athens as vice-consul, salary £400; 1821, when Greeks occupied Athens, left for island of Kea; after brief return, settled at Smyrna till death. MSS at Bibliothèque Nationale and Gennadios Library, Athens; précis of his journeys to 1802 and reports in *Proceedings* of Monuments and Antiquities section of Académie des Beaux-Arts; letters published in periodical *Magazin Encyclopédique*; map of Athens in atlas to Olivier's *Voyage* and Walpole's *Memoirs*, p 476; account of opening a tumulus in *Memoirs*, p 465; drawings in Choiseul's *Voyage*, Cousinéry's *Voyage* and Clarke's *Travels*; cf Ph. E. Legrand, *Rev Arch*, XXX (1897), pp 41 and 185ff, XXXI, pp 94 and 135ff. Acquisitions: see Chapters 1, 2 and 3.

tales in verse: *Ilderim, Phrosyne,* and *Alashtar,* 1816–17; also *Eastern Sketches,* 1819. Acquisitions: see Chapter 5, p 96.

Galt, John (1779–1839)   Alternated between business ventures and prolific writing; 1809–11, travelled Europe, Greece and Levant; of his many writings we cite only: *Voyages and travels, 1809–11,* 1812; *Letters from the Levant,* 1813; *Life of Byron,* 1830; *Autobiography,* 1833.

Gandy-Deering, John Peter (1787–1850)   Member of 1811 Dilettanti expedition; became well-known architect; contributed to Dilettanti, *Unedited Antiquities of Attica,* 1817. Acquisitions: part of a colossal head, a female torso and other fragments at Rhamnous, presented to BM in 1820; late fourth-century votive relief, bought by BM 1952.

Gell, Sir William (1777–1836)   On government mission 1801–2, visited Greece, Troad and Ionian Islands; 1805–6, travelled widely in Greece; 1811, led Dilettanti expedition to Greece and Levant; 1814, briefly chamberlain to Princess Caroline; from 1820, lived in Italy. *Topography of Troy,* 1804; *Geography and antiquities of Ionia,* 1807; *Itinerary of Greece, with a commentary on Pausanias and Strabo,* 1810; *Itinerary of the Morea,* 1817; *Narrative of a journey in the Morea,* 1823; works on Pompeii and Rome; MSS at Dept of Antiquities, BM.

Giraud family   Long-established merchants at Athens under French protection; a daughter married Lusieri, a son, Nicolo, was Byron's friend.

Gott, Benjamin   Travelled Levant and Greece with Rawson, died at the Piraeus 1815, buried in Theseion. Acquisitions: twelve Greek sepulchral marbles, altars and architectural fragments; Rawson preserved the collection, which was presented to the Museum of the Leeds Philosophical and Literary Society in 1863.

Graham, Sir Sandford, MP (1788–1852)   Travelled in Greece and Levant 1810–11, acquiring quantity of vases, see Chapter 3, p 70.

Gropius, Georg (*d* 1845 ?)   Entered service of W. von Humboldt in Rome where engaged by Aberdeen (or Bartholdy?) as artist to visit Greece; remained in Levant as merchant and agent for Aberdeen; 1810, English agent at Trichery, gulf of Volos; 1811, agent for sale of Aegina marbles, but dismissed for malpractice; 1812, helped excavate Bassae marbles; excavated and dealt in antiquities, partly in association with Fauvel; Austrian vice-consul at Athens about 1818; remained there or in Aegina throughout War of Independence.

Halgan, Amiral Emmanuel (1771–1852)   Fought in Napoleonic wars; served on French Levant station from 1819. Acquisitions: antiquities from Melos that went to Pourtalès collection, and see Chapter 3, p 70.

Haller, Baron Charles von Hallerstein (1774–1817)   Studied architecture at Nuremberg and Berlin for seven years; 1806, building inspector with private practice in Nuremberg; 1808, obtained leave to visit Italy; 1810, left for Greece with Brøndstedt etc; 1811, commissioned by Prince Ludwig of Bavaria to excavate and purchase antiquities; died in Thessalonika. MSS at Berlin, Strasbourg and Munich; letters to Cockerell at Dept of Antiquities, BM; diaries and letters published in *Grenzboten*, 1875 and 1876, *Kunstkronik*, 1875, *Zeitschrift für bildenden Kunst*, 1877 and 1883, all Leipzig. Acquisitions: see Chapters 6 and 7.

Hobhouse, John Cam (Baron Broughton; 1786–1869)   Friend of Byron, with whom travelled in Albania, Greece and Levant, 1809–10; entered politics, holding office, active on Greek Committee from 1823. *A Journey through Albania and Other Provinces of Turkey in Europe and Asia to Constantinople*, 1813 (1855 ed, 2 vols); *Recollections of a Long Life*, 1865. Acquisitions: two Aphrodites, now in BM; other marbles, including at least one head, now lost.

Holland, Sir Henry (1788–1873)   Travelled 1812–13 in Greece and Levant; became well-known doctor. *Travels in the Ionian Isles, Albania, Thessaly . . .*, 1815 (1819 ed, 2 vols).

Hughes, Rev Thomas Smart (1786–1847) After distinguished university career, appointed 1812–14 tutor to R. Townley Parker, touring Europe, Greece and Levant. *Travels in Sicily, Greece and Albania*, 2 vols, 1820 (amended ed 1830) with plates from drawings by Cockerell; *Address to the people of England in the cause of the Greeks* . . ., 1822; *Considerations upon the Greek Revolution*, 1823.

Hunt, Reverend Philip (*b* 1771) Appointed chaplain to Elgin's embassy to Constantinople 1799; at Athens 1801; 1803, taken prisoner with Elgin on return through France; held various livings, then Dean of Holkham, under new patron, the Duke of Bedford, for whom provided text for publication of Woburn marbles 1822. *Narrative of What Is Known Respecting the Literary Remains of the Late J. Tweddell*, 1816.

Huyot, Jean-Nicolas (1780–1840) Architect, accompanied Forbin on travels in Greece and Levant 1817–21; broke leg in theatre at Melos, lost papers in burning of Patras in War of Independence; Professor at École des Beaux-Arts, concerned with building Arc de Triomphe. MSS at Bibliothèque Nationale and RIBA.

Inwood, Henry William (1794–1843) Visited Greece 1819 to study Erechtheion in connection with construction of St Pancras New Church with his father, with whom continued to work in successful architectural practice. *The Erechtheion at Athens: Fragments of Athenian Architecture*, 1831; *The Resources of Design in Architecture of Greece, Egypt* . . ., 1834. Acquisitions: three fragments of votive reliefs and decorative relief from Laconia; fragment of sepulchral stele and decorative specimen from Mycenae; piece of stele from Athens; fragments from Erechtheion; helmeted head and votive relief, now in BM; it is not known what happened to Corinthian and Ionic capitals he acquired, see Chapters 2 and 3, pp 47 and 53.

Jenkins, William Travelled Greece with Donaldson, 1820; exhibited views of Athens at RA; contributed plates and explanations to 1830 volume of Dilettanti, *Antiquities of Athens*.

Kinnard, William (1788–1839) Travelled Italy, Greece and Levant 1818 with Eastlake and Barry; edited valuable 2nd ed of Vol IV of Dilettanti, *Antiquities of Athens*, 1825–30; contributed to 1830 volume of *Antiquities* (Athens and Delos).

Koes, G. H. C. (1782–1811) Danish scholar, travelled Italy and Greece with Brøndsted 1810; died at Zante.

Laurent, Peter Edmund (1796–1837) Classical scholar and language teacher; 1818–19, travelled Greece, Levant and Italy. *Recollections of a Classical Tour through Various Parts of Greece, Turkey and Italy*, 1821; Translation of Herodotus, 1827; *Introduction to Ancient Geography*, 1830.

Leake, Lt-Colonel William Martin (1777–1860) Member of 1799 military mission to Turkey, surveyed Egypt with Hamilton and Squire; 1802, at Athens, then in wreck of Elgin's ship *Mentor* at Cerigo; 1805, military and political mission to Morea; 1807, on English declaration of war on Turkey, detained nine months at Salonika; released to induce Ali Pasha to mediate; returned to England; 1808–10, mission to Ali; 1815, retired to arrange material collected on his journeys into his famous itineraries and publish coins acquired then and at English and continental sales. *Researches in Greece*, 1814; *Topography of Athens*, 1821; *Journal of a Tour in Asia Minor*, 1824; *An Historical Outline of the Greek Revolution*, 1825; *Travels in the Morea*, 1830 and *Peloponesiaca*, a supplement, 1846; *Travels in Northern Greece*, 4 vols, 1835; *Greece at the End of 23 years' Protection*, 1851; *Numismata Hellenica*, catalogue of his Greek coins, 1854, supplement 1859; *On Some Disputed Questions of Ancient Geography*, 1857. Acquisitions: torso of Apollo; two votive reliefs from Thessaly and one from Laconia; female torso and fragment of sarcophagus from Sparta; term with female bust from Mantinea; two terminal busts given to him by Ali Pasha, all presented to BM in 1839; collection of Greek coins, bronzes, vases, etc purchased after his death by Cambridge University for £5,000.

MacGill, Thomas Travelled in Levant 1803-6 as merchant; consul at Malta after 1811. *Travels in Turkey, Italy and Russia*, 2 vols, 1808.

Makri family Dr Macree, Scots doctor, settled in Athens marrying Theodorulla Mina c 1770; son Procopius (*d* 1799), known as Makri, was agent for Levant Company and cicerone to T. Hope; married 1794 Theodora Vretos, having three daughters, Marianna, Katinka and Theresa (Byron's 'Maid of Athens'); they married respectively Karkanides, a Zante captain, Pittakys, archaeologist, and Black, later consul at various Greek ports.

Marcellus, L. A. J. A. C. Demartin du Tirac, Comte de (1795–1861) Appointed secretary, French Embassy, Constantinople, 1815; responsible for acquisition of Venus de Milo; 1821, Secretary at Embassy, London; retired for political reasons. *Souvenirs de l'Orient*, 2 vols, 1829; *Épisodes littéraires en Orient*, 2 vols, 1851; *Chants du peuple en Grèce*, 2 vols, 1851; *Les Dionysiaques*, 1855, etc.

Masson family Nicholas, French-protected merchant, married 1787 to Greek lady; children emigrated to France before 1816; Haller, Stackelberg and Cockerell all stayed with Madame Masson in Athens.

Matterer, Capitaine de Vaisseau (1781–1868) Fought in Napoleonic wars, at Trafalgar; 1820, participated in discovery of Venus de Milo; later Major de la Marine, Toulon. Obituary of Dumont in *Annales Maritimes*, 1842; contribution in J. Aicard, *Recherches sur l'histoire de la découverte de la Venus de Milo . . .*, 1874.

Monck, Sir Charles (1779–1867) At Athens 1805, where wife had a child; built a house at Belsay, Northumberland, with assistance of Gell, incorporating features of Greek architecture; MP 1812-20.

North, Hon Frederick, 5th Earl of Guilford (1817) (1766–1827)
Received into Orthodox Church at Corfu 1791; 1798–1805,
Governor of Ceylon; 1811–12, travelled in Greece and Levant;
1814, President of Athens Philomousoi; devoted himself to
creation of university on Corfu, Regent 1819, Chancellor 1824;
resided at Corfu till death. Acquisitions: marble well-head, see
Chapter 3, p 57; part of sepulchral stele from Akharnae, presented BM 1886; other fragments from Olympia, etc have disappeared: he bequeathed them to University of Corfu but his
executors claimed them, they were shipped to England and
dispersed.

Page, William (working 1816–60) Artist, at Athens, probably
1818, then Levant and Rome; exhibited at RA; drawings in
Dilettanti, *Antiquities of Athens* and many unpublished at
Gennadios Library, Athens.

Poirot, Achille (1797–1852) Member of artistic section, Expédition de Morée 1829; became well-known historical painter.

Pomardi, Simone (1760–1830) Accompanied Dodwell to Greece
1805, making some 600 drawings. *Viaggio nella Graecia*, Rome,
1820.

Pouqueville, François C. H. L. (1770–1838) Medical member of
Commission accompanying Napoleon's invasion of Egypt;
1798, taken by pirates, made prisoner of war by Turks, held at
Tripolis whose surroundings he was allowed to survey; 1805,
appointed consul-general to Ali Pasha at Jannina; after initial
success, Ali turned anti-French and for nine years Pouqueville
was virtually a prisoner; 1816, returned to France to publish
his material. *Voyage en Morée, à Constantinople et en Albanie*, 3
vols, 1805; *Voyage de la Grèce*, 5 vols, 1820–2; *Histoire de la
Régéneration de la Grèce*, 4 vols, 1824.

Ravoisié, Amable (1801–69?) Member of artistic section of
Expédition de Morée 1829; from 1839, archaeological and
architectural missions in Algeria.

Rivière, Marquis Charles François de (1763–1828)   Émigré noble, captured and imprisoned; 1816–20, ambassador to Turkey; Venus de Milo purchased on his instructions for presentation to king.

Roque family   Nicholas from Carcassonne, merchant at Athens from about 1793; married Greek lady, perhaps sister of Makri's wife; son Focione went to Marseilles to study; daughter Félicité (Dudu) followed there during war, but died of broken heart.

Rottiers, Col Bernard E. A. (1771–1858) Dutch; 1808, fled to Russia, joining Imperial Army; 1818, resigned, returning home via Levant; 1825, on scientific mission to Levant for King of Netherlands, excavated at Melos and Rhodes. *Itinéraire de Tiflis à Constantinople*, 1829. Acquisitions: see Chapter 3, p 70.

Ruthven, James,   7th Baron (1777–1853) and wife, *née* Campbell (1789–1885)   At Athens 1818, excavated in land bought near Cape Zoster; presented collection, mainly vases, also two attic grave steles, to Edinburgh Antiquarian Museum (now Royal Scottish Museum), 1884.

Sligo, Marquess of (1788–1845)   Travelled in Mediterranean area 1809–11 and again 1815; Lord Lieutenant of Co Mayo 1831–3 and 1842–5; Governor-General of Jamaica 1833–6. Acquisitions: see Chapter 5, p 97.

Smirke, Sir Robert, RA (1781–1867)   Studied architecture in Italy, Sicily and Greece, with W. Walker, 1801–5; on return, built mainly in Doric and Ionic styles, eg British Museum. *Specimens of Continental Architecture*, 1806; MS travelogue and drawings, RIBA. Acquisitions: see Chapter 2, p 46, are now lost.

Society of Dilettanti   Founded 1732, evolved into notable supporter of expeditions and publications aimed at increasing knowledge of antiquity, exercising considerable influence on direction of contemporary taste. Cf *Historical Notices*, 1855, and L. Cust, *History of the Society of Dilettanti*, 1898.

Publications:

Antiquities of Athens, measured and delineated by J. Stuart and N. Revett; the Society presented 20 guineas to Stuart towards cost of Vol I, published 1762; after his death, it sponsored Vols II, ed W. Newton, 1787-90; III, ed W. Reveley, 1794-7; IV, ed J. Woods, 1814-16; and 2nd edition, ed W. Kinnard, 1825-30.

Antiquities of Athens and Other Places in Greece, Sicily, etc, supplementary to the above, delineated and illustrated by C. R. Cockerell (Agrigentum), W. Kinnard (Athens), T. L. Donaldson (Bassae, Messene, Mycenae), W. Jenkins (Athens) and W. Railton (Corfu), 1830.

Ionian Antiquities, published with the permission of the Society by R. Chandler, N. Revett and W. Pars, two parts, 1769 and 1797; parts III, 1840, IV, 1881, and V, 1915 (cf part II for Aegina, Sunion, Nemea and Eleusis); part I republished 1821 with additions and corrections as *Antiquities of Ionia*.

Unedited Antiquities of Attica, 1817, by W. Gell, R. P. Gandy, F. Bedford.

Two letters from Athens on Certain Anomalies in the Construction of the Parthenon, by F. C. Penrose, 1847.

Investigation into the Principles of Athenian Architecture, by F. C. Penrose, 1851.

Specimens of Antient Sculpture, Aegiptian, Etruscan, Greek and Roman, 2 vols, 1809 and 1835.

The Bronzes of Siris, by P. O. Brøndsted, 1836.

Expeditions: 1776: W. Chandler, N. Revett and W. Pars; 1811: W. Gell, R. P. Gandy, F. Bedford.

Stackelberg, Freiherr Otto Magnus von, of Estonia (1787-1837) Studied for diplomatic career but abandoned this for the arts; 1809, in Rome; 1810, to Greece with Haller, etc; despite illness, remained in Levant till 1814; 1816-23, in Rome, then to Paris, London, Dresden, St Petersburg. *Costumes et usages des grecques*, Vol I, Paris, 1824-6, Vol II, Berlin, 1837; *Der Apollotempel zu Bassae*, Rome, 1826; *La Grèce: vues pittoresques et topographiques*,

Paris, 1829, and Berlin, 1834; *Die Gräben der Hellenen*, Berlin, 1837. Cf biography by N. von Stackelberg, 1882. Acquisitions: see Chapters 6 and 7; personal collection mostly sold to Saxony, now in Dresden museums, cf catalogue published Dresden, 1837.

Stanhope, John Spencer Paroled by French 1813 to travel in Greece for archaeological research, particularly at Olympia, with architect Allason; at Athens 1814. *Topography of the Battle of Plataea* (dedicated to Institut de France), 1817; *Olympia*, 1824.

Stanhope, Lt-Colonel Leicester F. C. (Earl of Harrington 1851; 1784–1862) Visited Greece 1823 as agent of Greek Committee. *Greece in 1823 and 1824*, 1824.

Strangford, Percy Clinton Sydney, 6th Viscount (1780–1855) Diplomatic service in Portugal and Northern Europe; 1820–4, ambassador at Constantinople; then active as Tory peer and littérateur. Acquisitions: marble fragments including piece of copy of shield of Phidias' Athene, and Apollo from Anaphe, presented to Canterbury, retrieved for BM 1864.

Swan, Reverend Charles Chaplain HMS *Cambrian* from 1824. *Journal of a Voyage up the Mediterranean*, 2 vols, 1826. Acquisition: a bas-relief, perhaps lost in wreck of *Cambrian*.

Taylor, George L. (1788–1873) Visited Greece with E. Cresy, J. Sanders and artist W. Purser 1818. *Literary Gazette*, 24 April 1824; *Autobiography of an octagenarian architect*, 1870.

Trézel, Félix (1782–1855) Historical painter, first exhibited at Salon 1806; member of Expédition de Morée 1829, first archaeological then artistic sections; became well-known painter, specialising in Greek subjects.

Turner, William (1792–1867) Attached to Embassy, Constantinople, 1811–16 and 1824–9, travelling extensively in Ottoman Empire, 1812 with Tupper. *Journal of a Tour in the Levant*, 3 vols, 1820.

Tweddell, John (1769–99) Embarked on study tour 1795 via Northern Europe to Levant, where engaged Preaulx as artist; died at Athens, buried in Theseion by Fauvel; cf W. B. Dinsmoor, *Observations on the Hephaestion*, Boston, 1941. *Remains of J. Tweddell*, published by his brother, 2nd ed, 1816 (attacked Elgin for loss of his drawings, etc).

Voutier, O. (1796–1877) Joined French navy at fifteen; 1820, on Levant station, concerned in discovery of Venus de Milo; left service and in 1821 embarked with Gordon to join Greek forces in War of Independence. *Mémoires du col. Voutier sur la guerre actuelle des Grecs*, 1823 (discredited by Raybaud); *Découverte et acquisition de la Venus de Milo*, 1874.

Wagner, Johann Martin von (1777–1858) Studied in Vienna to become historical painter; 1804, in Rome, acquired Crown Prince Ludwig of Bavaria as patron; concerned in purchase of Aegina sculptures, visiting Greece 1811–12; sculpted internal frieze of Valhalla, 1822–37. *Bassorelievi del tempio di Apollo Epicurio in Arcadia*, Rome, 1814; *Bericht über die Aegenistischen Bildwerke* (with G. Schelling), Munich, 1817; Greek travelogue published by R. Herbig in *Würzburgen Fest. für H. Bulle*, Stuttgart, 1938. Acquisitions: collection bequeathed to University of Würzburg, including a Parthenon fragment.

Walpole, Reverend Robert (1781–1856) Classical scholar, travelled Greece and Levant 1806–8. *Memoirs relating to European and Asiatic Turkey*, edited from MS journals, 1817; continuation in *Travels in Various Countries of the East*, 1820. Acquisitions: vases, figurines, etc from tombs in Attica, presented to Cambridge University.

Wilkins, William, RA (1778–1839) Cambridge travelling bachelor 1800–4, visited Greece 1802 with artist Aglio; his design in Greek taste accepted for Downing College, Cambridge, 1804, partly constructed; prolific architect, Professor of Architecture RA 1837. *Antiquities of Magna Graecia*, 1807; *Atheniensia*, 1812 (folio 1816); *Civil Architecture of Vitruvius*, 1812 and 1817; *Prolusiones Architectonicae*, 1827 and 1837; drawings at RIBA.

ACKNOWLEDGEMENTS

I am indebted to the Victoria and Albert Museum for permission to reproduce illustrations; to the Council of the RIBA for permission to quote from the manuscript diary of Sir R. Smirke; to the Trustees of the British Museum for permission to use the Additional Manuscripts collection and the manuscripts in the Department of Greek and Roman Antiquities, whose Keeper, Mr D. E. L. Haynes, I would also like to thank. The London Library has been a source of much material. Acknowledgements are also due to the Martin von Wagner Museum in Würzburg for permission to use material from Wagner's travelogue and to the *Münchner Jahrbuch der bildenden Kunst* and the Staatliche Antikensammlungen, Munich, for permission to quote from J. Linckh's Aegina journal.

GENERAL INDEX